THE MIRACLE OF IRELAND

THE
MIRACLE
OF IRELAND

edited by
DANIEL-ROPS

Translated from the French by
THE EARL OF WICKLOW

HELICON PRESS INC.

Baltimore   Maryland

Library of Congress Catalog Card No. 59—6615.

Helicon Press 5305 East Drive, Baltimore 27. Md.

PRINTED IN THE REPUBLIC OF IRELAND BY CAHILL AND CO., LTD.,
DUBLIN FOR HELICON PRESS, INC. NIHIL OBSTAT : IOANNES
O'DONOGHUE. CENSOR THEOL. DEPUT. IMPRIMI POTEST. ✠IOANNES
CAROLUS, ARCHIDP. DUBLINEN, HIBERNIAE PRIMAS. DUBLINI
25 JUNE 1958.

CONTENTS

LIST OF ILLUSTRATIONS

The Miracle of Ireland

By DANIEL-ROPS of the Académie Française

THE history of Ireland during the dark ages is something astonishing and at the same time admirable. The ancient world had collapsed; Rome and her empire were no more than ghosts and nostalgic pictures. All over the West unchained violence had substituted for imperial order a chaos of darkness, of tears and of blood. Christianity, the only power that had survived the disaster, was trying to re-establish a civilization amid all this savagery, but in spite of the heroism of the saints, in spite of the firmness and wisdom of the bishops, what a difficult task the Church had before her, a task on which in fact the future of the world depended! It was then that, from a distant island, where faith in Christ was extraordinarily alive and active, from an island which had been protected from the risk of invasions, we should perhaps say protected by the intention of Divine Providence, men set out for the Christian conquest of the Continent, giving themselves up body and soul to this sublime and necessary work, and succeeded better than could have been hoped for plain human forces.

Yes, the history of this Celtic Christianity is astonishing and picturesque, bathed in poetry and mystery, battered by high winds and the spray of the sea; from those Northern mists which arise from the cold seas legends arise with the spontaneity of a dream, but from them there emerge many personalities with strange outlines, perfectly genuine, but with wondrous destinies. This is a history which has not always met with the notice it deserves, but anyone who studies it fairly will find it is of capital importance. "The Irish miracle" as we like to call it, is this second setting out of Christianity, from a country which had only just been baptised, and which was immediately dreaming of giving Christ back to the world. Ireland, between the fifth and the eighth century, was like a second Palestine, like a new cradle of the Christian faith. It seemed necessary to pay homage to this work, and here it is.

:-:   :-:   :-:

Ireland had remained outside the *Orbis romanus;* the legions had not trodden on her shores or planted their eagles there. The island

7

was little known by the ancient writers: one of their geographers,
Avienus, who wrote in the IVth century, called it the " sacred isle ",
words which no doubt revealed more ignorance than admiration. St.
Jerome spoke of its inhabitants in terms which were scarcely flatter-
ing, and repeats a ridiculous tale of cannibalism.   There is only one
exact note in the ancient writers: they had observed—no doubt
through the eyes of others—the verdant charm of the island, which
in our days has won for it the name of the " emerald isle ".   The
same Avienus tells us that " she spreads out her green plains on the
bosom of the waves " which makes an attractive line, for in those
happy days, geographers composed their treatises in the form of
poems. . . .

The origins of her Christian history are entwined with those of
other Celtic countries, and especially those of the islands facing her
and which two thousand years ago were inhabited by populations
related to her own.   Influenced by the spread of Christianity from
the third century onwards (there were three " British " bishops at the
Council of Arles in 314), and no doubt by the Orientals, who would
have come from the countries bordering on Persia, whether soldiers
or merchants arriving in the wake of the legions, the large island
of Britain already had a good number of the faithful when the
departure of the Roman soldiers, in 428, delivered up the Celtic
churches to the Anglo-Saxon invasion, that is to say to the horrors
which St. Gildas, the author of a tempestuous chronicle, describes in
a style like that of Jeremias.   Nevertheless these pursued branches
of Christianity had both resisted and survived: on these heroic
struggles were to be built up, on a mainly historical foundation, the
legendary cycle of King Arthur, dear to the medieval songs of heroic
deeds, and which we can find described even in the moulding of
the arches of the cathedrals.   Having taken refuge in the mountains,
these communities clustered around their monasteries and especially
around those twelve religious houses which St. David (+ 544), the
nephew of King Arthur, founded in Wales.   Indeed, life was not
easy for the British Catholics of those days, and it often happened
for a monastery to be so poor that the monks had to pull the plough
themselves.   But faith was a living thing and even passionate—
Always as passionate as in those days when Pelagius the Briton
argued interminably about grace, and when his doctrines had such
an attraction for souls drawn towards mysticism that it had been
necessary, in order to combat them, to send to the island St. Loup,
the Bishop of Troyes, formerly a monk of Lerins, and on two
occasions St. Germain of Auxerre.

Shortly after that disaster (round about the year 430), Ireland,
which was still, in the words of the chronicler Prosper of Aquitaine,

" a barbarous island ", became an object of care to Pope St. Celestine. He had sent a missionary Bishop, Palladius, to the Scots (as the Irish were then called), to whom Providence did not allow enough time to have any effect. But this same Providence was watching over the dear island in which little Christian nuclei must already have been in existence, probably from the Celtic Christian groups in Britain[1], of which several members had been able to seek refuge beyond the sea. Providence sent the man of God who was to make it into a bastion of Catholicism, and who is rightly regarded as the national hero—St. Patrick.

We shall soon be telling of the astonishing life of this young Briton who was carried away by a raid of Irish pirates, was kept for some time on the island—and this is the first aspect of the Irish miracle, that the Irish themselves went to fetch their apostle!—but managed to escape, returning later to this voluntarily, where he knew there were many good pagans, who were waiting for Christ. We shall see the famous St. Germain of Auxerre, listening to the young monk as he tells him of his vast plan, shewing confidence in him, consecrating him as a missionary bishop, and sending him out on this adventure. We shall consider those thirty years of almost tireless apostolate, during which, struggling by force of miracles against the cunning of the Druids, with an increasing number of sermons and missions, the great saint succeeded, without any clashes or violence, in substituting Christianity for the old Celtic religion, thus showing, in experimental fashion, that the Gospel is not only destined to be associated with Graeco-Roman civilization, but that it could also be adapted to every form of culture, and gave them a fresh vitality.

Another feature of the " Irish miracle " was thus this planting of Christianity in a country where Rome had not prepared the way. Nowadays, Irishmen are ready to proclaim that their national conscience is as St. Patrick formed it; their national feast-day is that of the great missionary bishop, and if the shamrock is to be found all over the island, in countless numbers, if it is reproduced on all the coats of arms, on so many walls, even on the aeroplanes of Aer Lingus, this is because, speaking on the rock of Cashel, Patrick compared the Trinity, three in one and one in three, to a humble three-leaved plant.

At the death of St. Patrick Ireland had so many Christian centres and so many monasteries that it could with justice be called " the island of the saints."

---

[1] We should remember that until the Vth century the word Britain only applied to Great Britain. It was only after the Bretons had installed themselves in Armorica that the peninsula of Armorica gradually took on the name of Brittany.

The island of the saints . . . where one still finds by chance along
the sunken roads such moving reminders of the most ancient history,
such as the awkwardly carved menhirs (monoliths) of the Christian
chrism.   The island of the saints, where in the middle of the
cemetries are to be seen the mysterious round towers which were
no doubt at the same time oratories, belfries, and turrets of defence
against Viking aggressors.   The island of the saints in whose calendar
are inscribed so many sonorous names which are unknown among
our French feast-days, Comgall, Brendan, Mochta, Killian, Benen,
Fiacre, Columba, Finnian.   The island of the saints where above
all there was literally a swarm of religious houses, which were to be
of the first importance for the future of Christianity.

The monasteries of Ireland soon became nurseries of the
missionaries and the adventurers of Christ: Killeany, Clonard, Clonmacnoise, Bangor, Glendalough, and many others.   Scarcely had it
been founded by St. Patrick, when the Irish Church evolved so
rapidly in the direction of monastic institutions, that the secular
element is scarcely seen.   Historians have asked themselves the reason
for this phenomenon which is no doubt not a miracle—let us make
the right use of the term—but which nevertheless remains extraordinary.   Alexandre Bertrand has produced the theory that Irish
monasticism was derived from the druidical communities: the monks
were no other than converted druids and like the druids they lived
in community . . . which remains to be proved, for this is no more
than a hypothesis like the whole system which Bertrand imagined.
Equally a hypothesis, and no more solid, is the theory which would
connect Irish with Egyptian monasticism.   Let us not seek for an
explanation, but be content with stating the fact.

The Irish were so given to see everything from the monastic angle
that for them the Pope was " the Abbot of Rome ", and Christ " the
Abbot of the Blessed in Heaven "   Their monasteries were regular
towns, sometimes containing as many as three thousand monks. Each
inhabitant had his hut and the whole was laid out like a camp.   Dom
Leclercq, who remains roguish and a little malicious beneath all his
erudition, compares these monasteries to molehills. But those who
inhabited them were not sedentary creatures like moles; they were
more like migratory birds.   The centre of the prayers and liturgy of
a clan, and also the real headquarters of ecclesiastical administration,
each of these monastic Bishoprics preserved around it a movement
of exceptional fervour.   Whilst culture was sinking in the West,
each of these centres was lighting a torch . . . a torch whose flame
would soon be carried everywhere.

:-:   :-:   :-:

The most striking characteristic of these Celtic monks was their love of journeys, of " roaming " for the sake of Christ. It is said that the Celts have always had a vagrant streak. What then was it like when combined with the passion for the apostolate! From these " British " communities buttressed against the Germans, from these young churches which had arisen in the steps of St. Patrick, missionaries were to set out, in an incredible number. " What was original," wrote Georges Goyau, " is that from the start of the spirit of evangelization one can see there is something more and better than the vocation of certain personalities; this spirit is aroused and sustained by a collective impulse of the Irish soul. The monasteries founded by St. Patrick were mission stations. Immediately, they contained the choicest souls, among whom the Christian creed had no halting-place; scarcely were they baptised when they wished to become monks, and it was in order to preach, to bring about more baptisms and to produce other monks."

The history of these "roamings" in the name of Christ is from every point of view a prodigy. The chronicles which give the accounts of them—of which all the details, it goes without saying, are not vouched for by strict historical criticism!—are full of unheard-of adventures in which there are monks who have taken a vow never to return to their native land, so that they may carry the Gospel everywhere, crews who embark on the sea without oars so that they may be the more abandoned to the will of God, to say nothing of stone troughs which miraculously become navigable ships and carry the saints whither Providence wishes them to be. The west coast of Great Britain and of what we now call Scotland, were to see religious houses arising from which the Gospel would radiate: Bangor and Chester, founded by St. Comgall, Kentigern in Scotland, founded by St. Ninian. Further, always further, towards the most unknown, the most formidable lands, all for the sake of Christ! Not content with having founded the abbeys of Durrow and Derry, in Northern Ireland, St. Columba, a former monk of Clonard, embarked round about the year 563 with twelve companions, converted the savage Picts, and founded on a tiny island on the southern corner of Scotland the monastery of Iona which was to be a nursery of bishops, a real Scottish metropolis from which the good news was to be carried to the Orkneys, the Shetlands, the Faroes (the *Ultima Thule* of the ancients) and even to Iceland. To what dangers, to what adventures (sometimes comical enough) these bold journeys led the monks, can be seen in the rich legends of St. Brendan the navigator which are still told by the fireside in Brittany, and are full of joyful or terrifying anecdotes; we hear of Masses said on the back of a whale which was taken for an island, and of the gates of Hell from which emerge,

amidst the ice, the fires of Polar Vulcans . . . this is mere legend.
When the Vikings discovered Iceland in the VIIth century, they were
to observe that the " Papas " of Ireland were already established and
that each island of the North Sea had its colony of ascetics.

Other ships set out in another direction, that of " new Britain ",
the Armorica to which the Anglo-Saxon invasion had, about the year
442, caused many clans to escape, and where the Celtic race was
to strike such vigorous roots that they would literally renew the
population.   Between the Celts of Great Britain and Ireland and
those of Armorica there survived, in spite of the distance, a direct,
constant and fraternal contact.   To speak the truth it was, and
continued to be for centuries, one single people on each side of the
grey sea, one single Christianity with the same characteristics, with
its own special customs, closely collected around these Bishopric-
monasteries; it would seem poetical and mystical in its outlook, and
with a disposition to travel.

This is when we must conjure up the Armorican epic of Celtic
monks who landed from the sea, that militia of the saints dear to
the hearts of the Bretons of France, that colonization of such a
special kind, of which geography and the names of places bear the
impress, and on which folklore continually feeds; St. Corentin, who
is said to have been the first Bishop of Quimper; St. Sanson, the
founder of Dol, for a long time the most important see in Brittany;
St. Paul Aurelian who sowed monasteries as he moved along, at
Onessant, on the island of Batz and in that country of Léon which
nowadays bears his name; St. Malo, the disciple of St. Brendan the
navigator; St. Brieuc, St. Tudual, St. Cadoc, St. Guénolé, and ever
so many others.   There is no Breton city which does not claim a
saint.   The most famous is perhaps St. Gildas, the son of a Breton
king, who having first of all come to Gaul in order to study, became
a monk, then later in Ireland wrote the history of his people; he
then returned to Armorica, disembarked—miraculously—on the
peninsula of Ruis, and while mixed up with all the history of the
Bro-Werec, managed to remain a man of contemplation in the midst
of activities.   It is true that everything in these fine saints' lives
cannot claim the dignity of history; but, even across the legendary
elements the main features of the beginnings of Christianity stand
out clearly: there was first the stage of installation, then the whole
country was taken in hand, favoured by the fact that the former
population were few in numbers, floating and with no organization;
then came a progressive and extraordinarily rapid extension, and the
Celtic Christianities of the islands served as reservoirs of men for
this conquest.   In two centuries the Celtic monks had really made
our Brittany which down to our days was never to lose the imprint

of its rough and fervent founders. There are also many Breton geographical names which date back to this Celtic and missionary conquest: *lann* means a hermitage, *plou* a parish (*plebs* in Latin, *pluwy* in Gaelic), *tré* a chapel of ease, etc.

And it was not only Brittany! Péronne became the centre of such an important Irish colony that it was known for a long time as *Perrona Scottorum,* while, quite close to Paris, Brie owed much to the Irish monks. The patron of Brie, St. Fiacre, was one of these. The first historian who has given in his writings some details about Brie is the Venerable Bede. Nicolas Vermualens, a professor of Louvain, published in 1639 a little book on the propagation of the faith in Belgium by the Irish; he gives the names of thirty-nine male and three female saints who came from Ireland to evangelize Belgium. The erudite think his list is too long, but is it not true that one lends only to the rich ? The Vosges, Alsace, Franche-Conté and Switzerland also owe much to them. We shall soon be reading, from the pens of Bernard Guillemain, Gonzague de Reynold, and Father John Ryan, some of the chapters of this prodigious history. To speak the truth, there is scarcely a country in the whole Christian West of the period which has not more or less borne the mark of these men, there is scarcely one which does not owe to them the awakening among their people of a faith which was to be that of the great Christian middle ages.

:-:   :-:   :-:

Of all these wanderers for Christ, all of whom had unusual destinies, the most extraordinary, the one who was to make the deepest mark, was that monk of Bangor who was seen disembarking at the little bay of Guimoraie, between Saint-Malo and Mont-Saint-Michel, one day in 575, with twelve companions—a granite cross still recalls the fact —and who, instead of remaining in Armorica, made for the forests of the East: St. Columban. A more detailed account of his life will be given in the study made of him and his valour by Mlle. Marguerite Dubois: a picturesque life if ever there was one. Born in Ireland in 540 he was in his young days such a wonderful youth that he became embarrassed by the constant female glances at his face. " There is only one salvation for you," said a holy recluse, " flight "; he fled. When he had spent some years at Bangor practising the prodigious mortifications that we know were the custom there, and to which he added to suit his own taste, the young adolescent, with fair hair and fresh complexion, was scarcely to be recognized in the bearded gnarled giant, with muscles of steel, who could fell a tree with one blow of an axe, and worked for fifteen hours moving earth without any apparent fatigue. He was a rough man, all right, who disembarked

at Guimoraie.   A sort of prophet of Israel brought back to life in the
sixth century, as blunt in his speech as Isaias or Jeremias, on whose
face, so his biographer tells us, " the strength shone visibly," a walker,
a preacher, an indefatigable clearer of the ground, a healer and more
or less a seer, in whom the old influence of Ireland had left its trace
of poetry and mystery, the love of nature and of dreaming.

Let us picture this Elias, this Isaias, this John the Baptist of the
sixth century, with his companions of the mission; this gnarled giant,
whose wrists were said to have subdued bears, was setting out into
this strange land followed by a band of monks, like him champions
for the truth, and like him tonsured in the Celtic manner, with
long hair falling onto the shoulders, but shaved in front like the half
of a crown.   They carried the long staff of a pilgrim; from the haver-
sacks which they carried they would draw out their liturgical books
and their little packets of relics, and they would start to speak.   No
human glory impressed them, whether that of king or bishop, not
even the councils which, when they had been summoned, they declined
to attend.   They proclaimed the need for penance, and denounced
sins and crimes in emphatic terms.   For almost fifty years, at the
turn of the sixth century, souls were stirred by the influence of St.
Columban.   His passing through the country started a real contagion
of holiness.

Crossing Gaul, from the west to the east, Columban wandered for
several years, clearly without any definite plan—this wandering by
chance at the behest of Providence is characteristic of his ways—till
the day when, in the region of the Vosges, the King of the Burgundians
offered him a place where he could establish himself, a place where
the land and the inhabitants were equally wild.   This was his first
foundation: Annegray, which was soon famous throughout the
countryside, and was soon besieged by the thousands of sick people
who were attracted by the gifts of the thaumaturge, was also soon too
small for the quantity of monks who sought admission.   In 590,
on the site of a little town of Gaul which had been burnt by Attila,
Columban founded Luxeuil which was to become, for several centuries, a high place of the spirit in Eastern France, a sort of French
Monte Cassino.

It is difficult to imagine the prestige of this monk in his time, for
twenty-five years.   People came from all sides in order to consult him;
kings venerated or feared him; the Gallo-Roman or Frankish bishops
viewed him with a respectfully anxious eye . . . we must wait for
St. Bernard to find such a dominant position in France.   When he
left his monastery and visited a province, vocations sprang up beneath
his feet: Adan and Ouen, two brothers, founded Jouarre and Rabais
(Ouen is the St. Ouen of the Parisians), while Fare, a young girl

of noble family, in opposition to her family, adopted Columban's hard rule and founded Faremoutiers. Nothing could hold this man back, neither difficulties nor respect for the powers that be. Because he spoke out openly to King Thierry, a man of criminal and base habits, and steadfastly refused to bless his bastards, Columban, who had thought at one moment that he would be killed, was finally driven out of Luxeuil, banished from the kingdom, and could only return there in disguise. What matter! However painful was the parting with his sons, were there not souls to be saved elsewhere, to be won for the Lord ? It was the Rhenish lands who were to see him next, those Rhenish lands where the passage of the invasions had left many souls in a barbarian state, Coblenz, Mainz, Basel where his disciple Ursanne settled, Arbon on the lake of Constance, Bregenz at the foot of the Arlberg where he founded a second Luxeuil. Then, since King Thierry still threatened to pursue him, the saint passed by the lake, to the south; his disciple, St. Gall, was taken ill, halted and immediately founded at Steinach the famous abbey which bears his name. After going down into Italy, Columban founded yet another monastery on the Trebbia, at Bobbio, when death at last allowed him to take a little rest (615). Such an existence, entirely occupied with the desire to spread the word of God, resting on the solid bastion of the monasteries, is characteristic of this great story.

The influence of the Irish monk was to be an abiding one; what a number of saints were to come from his abbeys, such as St. Philibert, the founder of Jumièges and Noirmoutier, St. Mommelin of Noyon, St. Ower, St. Bertin! And the special stamp which he had imprinted on the Christian soul is to be found again in his pupils, such as St. Wandrille, the founder of Fontenelle; it has been estimated that two hundred abbeys came to birth through his influence. There are many places, in the whole of the West, which bear his name or its variants. Above the Rhone, for example, at Culoz, a magnificent mountain, which Paul Claudel has compared to a crouching lion, still bears the name of the saintly Irish missionary.

:-:   :-:   :-:

The action of these conquerors for Christ must not only be considered in its extent, for it went very deep and did much to give to medieval Catholicism, as it would be when it emerged from the Barbarian chaos, the characteristics that we know. The prodigious developments of the monastic institution, which was the mark of Celtic Christianity thanks to the Irish missionaries, was extended to the whole of the West. The houses following St. Columban's rule, which were seen arising in the steps of the apostle, for a long period experienced a considerable development, and communities were to be found on the Continent with a thousand monks. But there was also a sort of influence, *a contrario;* in developing, Irish monachism aroused a kind of holy rivalry, especially when the rule of St. Benedict began to spread, and the order derived from the patriarch of Nurcia began to propagate itself. It was to a large extent in order to counter-balance the Columbanian current from Luxeuil that other abbeys were founded, following different rules, as when St. Éloi and Dagobert founded Saint-Denis near Paris. Irish monachism had gradually to merge into the great Benedictine current: the rule of St. Benedict, which was less rigorous, became more popular, but that of St. Columban did not disappear entirely from the Continent and it continued to survive in the island.

It is that — and this is one of the features which marked the originality of Irish Christianity—St. Columban's rule (and in general all the observances of Irish monasteries) laid special stress on penance, while that of St. Benedict insisted rather on the divine office. True enough, the Irish monasteries were also homes of prayer, and they also practised the *laus perennis,* as certain Byzantine monasteries had conceived it and held it in honour. But penance was the essential thing, and it was conceived by these rough warriors for God in a way that would be nowadays very disturbing to the rank and file of the faithful, and even the rank and file of the monks! The rule of St. Columban makes use of the scourge with unsparing liberality: six strokes for the monk who has forgotten to answer " Amen ", ten for the one who gashes the table with his knife, six for whoever sings out of tune, and right up to two hundred for serious offences! In the ordinary course of life, fasts, corporal penance, and various penalties are the normal thing. The penances were accepted, some even added on to them, like the Irish saint who was known to chant all the psalms standing in freezing water.

It can be imagined that these austere and painful practices were not without their influence on the faith of the Christian flock. It was in order to guide confessors that the *penitentials* were drawn up which Gabriel Le Bras studies in this volume in such a lively fashion, these " tariffs of penalties applicable to every type of sin ", these " ladders of failings and difficulties " which are so curious to consider. It is clear that the Irish penitentials " have in view the social and moral condition of a people which is still semi-pagan "; it has also doubtless been observed that this automatic quality of the punishment seems to neglect the interior dispositions of the culprit and the inner qualities of the offence: it is no less true that the practice of frequent confession, if frequently repeated, tends to refine the Christian conscience, to assign a great rôle to directors of conscience; even when mediocre, these penitentials have had the merit of making clear

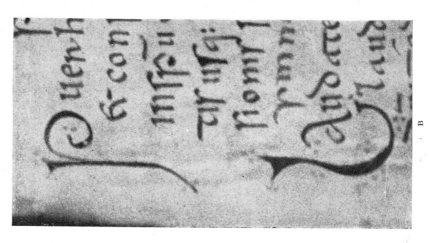

B

A

I (A) A pillar at Kildun, Co. Mayo. — I (B) Details of a page of the antiphonary of Bangor (Ambr. C.S. inf.).

A

B

C

2 (A) An ecclesiastic holding a cross and a bell at Killadeas, Co. Fermanagh.
2 (B) Bell of St. Gall in the Cathedral of St. Gall.
2 (C) Bell of St. Godeberte in the Cathedral of Noyon.

the faults to be avoided, and the Gospel ideal which should be followed.

We can thus see that there was a real Irish spirituality, which is studied in this volume by Father Fulbert Cayré—which, like all great schools of spirituality follows a curve, first of all in a full state of development, then, after reaching the heights, declining. But this spirituality which met later with that of the great middle ages, preserved its characteristic features throughout the centuries. We know of the relations which existed—Alexandre Masseron here reminds us of them—between St. Bernard of Clairvaux and the illustrious Irish saint of the XIIth century, St. Malachy: on the other hand, it was only from the moment when the Cistercians installed themselves in Ireland that the rule of St. Benedict was substituted completely for those of St. Columban and the Celtic monks of old, the rule of St. Benedict as strictly interpreted, in the tradition of Citeaux and the White Monks.

It goes without saying that this strictly religious action was combined with an intellectual influence, for at that epoch—and indeed during all the middle ages, there was no literary or artistic activity conceived outside the Church and the Christian framework. The Irish had a share in the literary culture of the West, a share which is studied here by Mgr. René Aigrain. The metrical compositions of St. Columban (of which we shall read an example) who was not without some inspiration from Virgil, bear witness to this, and when reading the Venerable Bede's *Ecclesiastical History of the English Nation*, one is struck by the homage which he frequently pays to the culture of the Irish, notably in biblical matters, where their influence seems to have been considerable. In another domain, that of Canon Law, the same influence is to be found, which is all the more interesting in that the legal traditions of the Irish Church were not derived, as were others, from Roman Law, but from ancient British traditions. It was from the "Romanisation" of these canonical traditions that there emerged the famous collection called *Hibernensis* which must have had a considerable circulation, even on the Continent. Later, in the Carolingian era, the intellectual influence of the Irish would be quite definite: at Laon, at Rheims, at Liège, and in many other places, and for several centuries, there would be Irish teachers of whom John Scotus Eriugena—which means " son of Ireland "—would be the most renowned; it has been possible to query his theological theses but not without their shedding light.

It remains to be said that Ireland's share in Western culture was no less interesting in the world of art, but we had better leave this specialized subject to Mlle. Francoise Henry, in which she has gained an authority contested by nobody, and whose study, a little later on, is so rich in original matter. This " Hibernian " art, which is so little known on the Continent, strikes the visitor to Ireland with astonishment. Those " Gaelic crosses " are not at all what one sees in France or in Italy; those manuscripts are ornamented with mysterious geometrical designs which are subtly thronged with fantastic animals and monsters out of a dream. Whence does this art come, from what immemorial origins ? How and why did it exercize a certain action on the Continent ? How also and why did it maintain itself, at the time of the great Roman expansion followed by the Gothic, apart from and as if following on the art of Chartres and of Rheims ? These are fascinating themes for study, and are perfectly set out by the University College lecturer. One is tempted to dream before the pictures which she provides of fine examples of this art . . .

:-:   :-:   :-:

For a long time, throughout the centuries, and especially through the agency of the religious houses which came from them, the West knew what it owed to these Irish missionaries, thanks to whom the Gospel had been sown once again, in the old land of Europe, after the rough ploughing up of the Barbarian invasions. Does it still know this today ? Not sufficiently. And yet we can ask ourselves if our countries would have been Christian as they were at the time of the cathedrals and crusades, if there had not been, years before, at the period of clearing and exploration, those pioneers from the island who traced out the way for the future builders. The " Irish Miracle " is an important element in Christian history ; that is why it seemed necessary and right to present it here under its chief aspects.

Saint Patrick and the Christian Origins of Ireland

By CHANOINE CHRISTIANI

Honorary doyen in the Faculty of Letters
of the Institut Catholique of Lyons

Before Saint Patrick.

THE Christian origins of Ireland are surrounded with shadow, as are those of all countries which are situated geographically like the ancient Erin. In the oldest known times it was peopled by small brown stocky men of the race known as Ligurian or Mediterranean, and which was dominant in Western Europe during the neolithic era, but it was invaded and conquered by the Celts, who were to become known as the Scots, round about the VIIIth century before Jesus Christ. This new race of tall blond men still constitutes the foundation of Irish population. And the Scots had naturally brought with them their deities, which were to drive back those of the Ligurians. Traces of the struggles which took place are to be found in the old legends of the country, notably in the victory of Partholon over a band of obscure and infernal gods, who were no doubt mediterranean gods.

The pagan Irish, after the arrival of the Scots, worshipped deities like those of the continental Celts: Dana and Bilé, a pair who gave birth to others; Lir, a god of the sea; Lug, the god of light, who reminds us of Lugdunum (Lyons) in Gaul; Ogma, the god of speech and eloquence; Angus, the goddess of love; Brigit, the goddess of poetry and wisdom, the counterpart of Minerva or Athene. A priesthood of druids, as in continental Gaul, practised at the same time medicine and divination, and controlled the instruction of youth.

What we do not know is how Christianity made its appearance in Ireland. Ireland did not lie on one of the great commercial routes, she was enveloped in her legends as in the fogs of her soft damp climate. The country was divided into clans, which was very favourable for mass conversions. It is probable that it happened to Ireland as it happened elsewhere, but that which specially happened, which we shall see later on, was with St. Patrick. The Scots, many of whom were bold pirates, readily went to make raids on the neigh-

bouring coasts of Britain, perhaps also of Gaul. Foreigners, who had
been reduced to slavery, or sailors and traders coming in from outside, may have been the harbingers of Christianity. Everything there
in the religion of the Gospel that was gentle, just, and full of
hope, that had the great dream of a happy immortality, was already
able to attract the sons of Erin. But these are no more than frail
conjectures.

We only reach the solid soil of history towards the end of the
first third of the Vth century. There is a mention, unfortunately
all too short, but the authenticity of which nobody holds in doubt,
to be found in the year 431, in the Latin *Chronicle* of St. Prosper of
Aquitaine, on the subject of the evangelization of the Scots. Pope
St. Celestine I would have sent at that date a missionary called
Palladius " to the Scots who believe in Christ ". Legend attempted
after this to embroider this precious piece of information, but it did
so with so many obvious anachronisms, that we cannot hope to draw
from it anything definite or valuable. If, however, we analyse
Prosper's statement, we have the idea that Palladius was sent as
bishop to a flock which was already in existence. The Pope conferred
on him the episcopal dignity to govern " those of the Scots who
already believe in Christ ". How many were there ? It is impossible
to say, but there is no doubt that Palladius had to organize a Church
which was already half formed.

Unfortunately he died about a year after his arrival in Ireland.
He thus did not have the time to do anything. From 432 onwards
another missionary enters the scene. He would have to start everything over again, everything to build up. He was to do it so success-
fully, he was to leave such a memory, that it is with him we must
connect, without hesitation, the whole of Christian history in its Irish
origins. That apostle was Saint Patrick, and this has been recognized
by men of learning since the XVIIth century. In the first place
of those who have studied the question we must place the Niçois
Frenchman Antoine Pagí (1624-1699), who has said of Patrick: " It
is to him that the Irish owe the fact that their country has become
the *Island of the Saints* and even, during our time, the centre of
influence in letters and sciences." It is therefore with St. Patrick
that the brilliant Christian origins of Ireland are closely linked. The
island had not however lost the memory of Palladius, " first bishop
of the Scots ", and his feast was celebrated in the ancient Scottish
liturgy on July 6th.

Saint Patrick.

The greatness of St. Patrick is reflected in two convergent groups
of facts: on the one hand, his name was so famous that legend

never ceased to embellish his work, just as it was to flourish with us (French) around St. Martin and later Charlemagne. And on the other hand he managed to transform Ireland so powerfully that it became, also after him, as we may say, a land of monks, of nuns, of saints. If we would speak of him, we cannot do better than to quote him himself as much as possible. It will be the way by which we can remain on the most certain and at the same time the most stirring ground of history. We have the good fortune to have two writings of his, the authenticity of which is considered to be beyond dispute, his *Confession* or the account of his life by himself and his *Letter to the Christian Subjects of Coroticus*. It is from the first of these valuable documents that we shall borrow most: —

Birth, Captivity, Escape.

" I, Patrick," he writes, " the most unlearned, and least (the most humble) of all the Faithful, the most despicable also of all the multitude, had for my father the deacon Calphurnius, the son himself of a priest named Potitus who lived in the village of Bannavem Taburnial, and possessed a small property—villulam—nearby. And it was there that I was taken prisoner."

At one time the most widespread opinion placed the birthplace of our saint at Dumbarton, on the estuary of the Clyde. The date of his birth is unknown. It must be round about the year 389. About the year 404 a band of Irish pirates invaded the country where Patrick lived and he was taken away as a captive, then sold as a slave.

" I was," he says, " about sixteen years old. I knew nothing of the true God, and I was taken into Ireland into captivity along with several thousand other men. We were punished according to our deserts, for we were estranged from God, and we no longer obeyed our priests, when they instructed us for our salvation. The Lord thus made us conscious of His anger and His reprobation. He dispersed us among the nations, as far as the extremities of the earth, to those places where my small efforts still have some effect among strangers. But there, the Lord opened the senses of my unbelief, so as eventually to make me remember my sins, so that I might be converted with my whole heart to God. He gave a glance of pity at my wretchedness, at my youth and my ignorance. He preserved me before I was even aware of it. At that time when I was not able to distinguish between good and evil, He came to my help and consoled me as a father does with his child! . . ." Patrick's youth, in spite of the title of deacon borne by his father, must thus have been abandoned and neglected. He had lived, without care for goodness or for sin, knowing only very little about God. But the ordeal of his captivity was for him the road of salvation. He thought

and he began to pray. In his trouble he had no other confidant but
God. In touching lines his *Confession* bears witness to the infinite
divine mercy.

"Every day," he writes, "after my arrival in Ireland, I kept flocks.
And often, during the day, I used to pray. More and more, the love
of God grew in me and also the fear of His name. My faith was
increasing. I offered up as many as one hundred prayers in the day
and at night, almost as many. In the forests and on the mountains,
I woke up before the dawn in order to pray, in the snow, the frost
and the rain. I paid no attention to any fatigue. No laziness, if I
judge rightly at this time, held me in bondage, for my spirit was
overflowing with fervour.

"One night, in my sleep, I heard a voice, and it said to me: 'You
fast well—you will soon go to your own country.' Then, at the end
of some time, I once again heard a voice which said to me: 'Here
is your ship all ready.'

"But the sea was a long way off; it was perhaps two hundred miles
to the port. I had never been there and knew nobody there. But
I resolved to run away and I left the man with whom I had been
for six years."

We are thus round about the year 410. Patrick at that time knew
nothing of human letters, and little enough of divine things. The
prayers which came back to memory, in his distress, were assuredly
the most elementary ones known to a Christian; the *Pater Noster*
first of all, then the *Credo*, perhaps a few fragments of the psalms.
But his prayer, poor though it was in words, was all the more intense
and continual. This feature remained dominant all through his
life. Patrick was eminently a man of prayer, which means a man
who lives in God, with God, and by God.

"By the strength of God," he says, "I found my way under His
guidance. I feared nothing till I reached the port. On the very day
of my arrival, the ship was ready to leave. I asked the captain to
take me with him, but he pushed me aside and cried out indignantly:
'Don't you try and come with us!' At these words, I left them
to return to the hut where I was staying; as I walked along I was
praying, and before my prayer was finished, I heard someone crying
out with all his force from behind: 'Come quickly! Those people
are calling for you!' I immediately went back towards them, and
they said: 'Come, for we will take you on in good faith, make
friends with us, as you please.'

"I did not enter into intimate friendship with them for the fear
of God. But I hoped they would come in the faith of Jesus Christ
because they were pagans. However I remained with them and we
started immediately."

After a crossing that lasted three days, the ship which was carrying Patrick reached the land. He does not state which country it was, but it must surely have been Gaul. However, it seems that the navigators landed in a wooded place where, in a state of complete bewilderment, they moved in a circle without finding their way to the inhabited areas. Anyway, that is how we understand the next part of Patrick's account.

" For twenty-eight days," he writes, " we made our way through the wilderness. Eventually all failed us and hunger began to torment us. One day, the captain said to me: ' What is it you claim, Christian ? That your God is great and all-powerful ? Why then do you not pray for us, who are in danger of dying of hunger ? From now on we have little enough chance of seeing any men.'

" As for me, I replied: ' Be converted with all your hearts to the Lord your God, for nothing is impossible to Him, and even today He can send you some food, enough to fill you, for everywhere He has it in abundance.'

" And, thanks be to God, the thing happened. A herd of pigs appeared. They killed many of them and remained two days feasting on them . . . then, they gave thanks to God and I was held in honour among them."

From then on there was no shortage of food. They offered Patrick some wild honey. He said to himself: " This has been immolated " —which means " offered to idols ". He refused to eat any of it.

" The same night," he continues, " during my sleep, I was strongly tried by Satan, to a point that I shall never forget as long as I live. And he fell on my chest like an enormous rock, and I could no longer move any of my limbs. But I do not know where the thought came from to invoke Elias! Suddenly I saw in the sky the sun rising and I started to cry out with all my strength, ' Elias, Elias!' All at once the splendour of the sun fell on me, and I no longer felt the weight which was crushing me. And I think that I was then aided by Christ Jesus and that it was His spirit which was crying out in me, as I hope that He will do it again in the day of my judgment . . .!"

This " second captivity " of Patrick lasted for two months. Once again some years passed by and Patrick returned to Great Britain and saw his parents, who received him as a son. We can place this event about the year 415. He was thus about twenty-four years old.

The Call of Ireland.

His parents begged him to leave them no more, after all that he had suffered. But he had a vision which altered the whole course of his life from then onwards.

" One night," he said, " I saw coming to me a man named

Victoricius. He brought me an innumerable quantity of letters. And I read at the head of one of them these words: ' Voice of the Irish '. And while I was reading out loud the beginning of this letter, I seemed to hear the voice of those who lived near the wood of *Foclut,* which is near to the Western sea. And they all said at the same time: 'We beg you, holy young man, to come and to live again amongst us!' And I was extremely moved in my heart, and I could not read any more. And I woke up. Thanks be to God, at the end of seveal years, their prayers were heard."

"At the end of several years " Patrick has just told us. We must understand that he had to prepare himself for the great apostolic mission to Ireland, with which he seemed to be charged. His *Confession* unfortunately tells us nothing definite on the subject of this necessary formation. But certain sure signs point towards Gaul.

Patrick talks continually of his " Gallic friends ". He is writing his *Confession* for them, and for very numerous sons—thousands, he says, whom he has baptized in the Lord in Ireland. He humbles himself for his small knowledge of Latin letters, comparing his ignorance with the deep knowledge of those who " have drunk in the sacred letters and have perfected their language, changing in nothing since their childhood ", while for him " Latin was a foreign tongue ".

There can be no doubt that Patrick learnt everything he knew of Latin and of the sacred scriptures in Gaul. He must have stayed there from the year 415, which was that of the call in a dream towards Ireland, till his return to that island, about the year 432. Taking then everything which seems probable in the later biographies of St. Patrick—that of Tirechau, towards the end of the VIIth century, and that of Muirchu, which is the first to supply a regular composition —we roughly come to this conclusion:—

Patrick probably frequented the great Gallic monasteries of his time, those of Marmoutiers near Tours, and of Lérins, on the shores of the Mediterranean. There is no other explanation why he propagated the monastic life in Ireland with so much zeal and success.

But he had, above all, the grace of meeting in Gaul an eminent master in the person of Saint Germanus of Auxerre. The reputation of Saint Amator and of Saint Germanus of Auxerre, his successor as the bishop of that city, is enough to explain the presence of Saint Patrick near them. He seems to have been instructed in the Bible by Saint Amator, and to have been ordained deacon by him. But Amator died in 418, and it was Germanus who completed Patrick's ecclesiastical formation. One might say that his " seminary period " lasted from 415 to 432. He acquired above all what was then re- garded as essential, a profound knowledge of the Scriptures. He constantly quotes them in his writings. And he quotes them in the old Latin version, previous to St. Jerome's Vulgate, which is a clear guarantee that his *Confession* and the *Letter to Coroticus* are authentic. We may also consider it as highly probably that Saint Germanus, when he went to Great Britain in 429, under orders from the Pope, to combat the Pelagian heresy, accompanied by Saint Lupus of Troyes, took Patrick with him, since he himself was a Briton. It also is probable that Germanus and Patrick learnt of the death of Palladius, in 431, and that they decided the time had come to take up his succession and to pursue the task which he had scarcely had time to sketch out.

The Apostle of Ireland.

What is certain is that Patrick returned to Ireland about 432 and that he worked there without a break till his death, which is estimated to have taken place about the year 461. He had received episcopal consecration before his departure, perhaps from Saint Germanus himself, or from Pope Saint Celestine, or from Saint Maximus of Turin. But he went as a missionary bishop, without the title of any See. The most certain tradition ascribes to him the foundation of the See of Armagh, but only about 445, some thirteen years after he disembarked in Ireland, perhaps after a visit to Pope Saint Leo the Great.

His first landing took place, it is believed, at the mouth of the Vartry river (in ancient times the Dee), not far from the town of Wicklow, where Palladius had landed the previous year. It is impossible to follow with any certainty the route he followed in the island. He evangelized especially the regions of the north and centre and also the county of Limerick in the south.

We cannot have perfect confidence in the more or less romanticized accounts which came into circulation in the biographies of a poor period, but it is easy to disentangle some authentic texts:— (1) the nature of the struggles which he had to undergo; (2) the ways and methods which he employed in his apostolate.

He had to fight especially against the druids, the priests of the pagan religion which held sway in the island. A passage in his *Confession* proves they, above all, worshipped the sun. To this cult he skilfully opposed that of the "true Sun, Jesus Christ, who will never die!" He had, he said, to confront Kings. On a number of occasions he was thrown into prison, but on each occasion the Lord delivered him.

His tactics, which were very adroit, consisted in making a direct approach to the Kings of the different peoples. He used to debate in their presence, and used to affirm with definiteness that the adorers of the visible sun would be punished by God. As he had a thorough knowledge of the language of the country, and as he was very well versed in the scriptures, he had no difficulty in confounding the druids with the brilliance of his speech, with biblical images, and the promises of eternal salvation which were brought by Jesus Christ. Once the local King was converted, the whole people followed his example. From that there came mass conversions by means of which Ireland was completely transformed.

It would be false only to draw attention to Patrick's natural gifts, his indomitable courage, his eloquence, his biblical knowledge. He counted far more on *prayer* and *penance*. Patrick was a *giant of prayer* and a *giant of penance*. In his *Confession* he could take credit that he had never accepted anything from his converts, that he had redistributed everything which was given to him, that he had never dreaded prison or death, nor slavery, that in all things he had practised the most complete abandon to God, that he was always ready to shed his blood for Jesus Christ.

Legend has endowed Saint Patrick with marvellous exploits, giving highly improbable figures, such as that of the three hundred and sixty-six bishops he is supposed to have consecrated in Ireland. The reality is actually much finer. Alone, with the help of God, he conquered whole " peoples ", recruited clerics, baptized thousands of heathen, and founded monasteries. Let us listen to him humbly giving thanks to God for the work accomplished:

" I am," he says, in his *Confession*, " greatly a debtor to God in that He has granted me such a great grace making numerous peoples to be reborn to God through me, and that they have afterwards been led to the fulness of Christianity; and also that clerics have been ordained everywhere to govern the multitude who have recently come to the faith and whom the Lord has conquered from the extremities of the earth, as He had promised."

He quotes here a very large number of prophetic texts drawn from the Gospels and the Scriptures of the Old Testament.

" So that," he continues, " the Irish who had never had any knowledge of God, but who up to this day honoured impure idols, how then have they become the people of the Lord and are called the sons of God ? *The sons of the Scots and the daughters of the kings are now, for all to see, the monks and virgins of Christ !*"

This last sentence is to be found on two occasions in the short writings of Saint Patrick. He tells how a young girl of noble family, of great beauty, who was baptized by him, declared to him that she had received a communication from Christ that she was to become a virgin of Christ and consecrate herself to God. Her parents indignantly opposed this plan, but nothing could dissuade her and her example was followed by a great number of young girls of the Irish race.

One eventually finds, in Saint Patrick's *Confession,* this impressive phrase: " *By my ministry the Lord has had pity on thousands of thousands.—Et misertus est mihi Dominus in millia millium.*" Patrick thus converted the Irish by the thousand, if not by the million! He must surely be placed in the first rank of the great missionaries of Christian history.

In the legend of Saint Patrick, we must here recall what is known as the saint's " purgatory ". This legend goes back to the English monk, Henry de Saltrey, about 1190. He tells us that the saint, who wished to destroy the incredulity of the Irish on the subject of sufferings in the next life, was led by the Lord into a cavern which communicated with Hell. Whoever remained there for one day and one night with faith would receive the pardon of all his sins, and if he persevered in a good life, eternal life. This cavern is on an island of Lough Derg (Lake of the Cavern), in Ulster. It is still a place of annual pilgrimage from June 1st to August 15th. Pilgrims stay there three days, giving themselves up to various austerities, and to this day the Irish go there in thousands.

The Heritage of Saint Patrick.

However, the heritage left by Saint Patrick to his dear Irish is not derived merely from legend. His finest crown was the galaxy of saints associated with his name and his glory. We will only speak of those who were nearest to him and in the front rank of these is Saint Mel. He would have been the son of Conis and of Darerca, Patrick's sister, and he would have had for brothers, Melchu and Muinis, both of whom are equally honoured as saints. When Patrick founded, perhaps, in 445, the episcopal See of Ardagh, he installed as Bishop and superior of the monastic house his nephew Mel, who had remained the patron of the diocese, and whose feast falls on February 6th.

But what we must not forget, is that everywhere else in Ireland Bishoprics were established, following close upon Patrick and in similar conditions. A number of these churches afterwards became monasteries! From the beginning, the clergy in every church or monastery were trained by Patrick in practices of prayer and penance of a quite special character and which are to be found nowhere else in that form, which Patrick would seem to have invented.

In the Roman Breviary we read, on March 17th, St. Patrick's feast day, the following lesson, which will help us to understand what goes before: —

" Apart from his daily care for the churches, he never relaxed his invincible spirit of prayer. It seems to be certain that each day he recited the complete Psalter, with the Canticles and Hymns and that he added to this two hundred prayers. Every day he worshipped God three hundred times with genuflections and during each canonical hour he made the sign of the cross one hundred times. He divided the night into three periods, devoting the first to the recitation of one hundred psalms, accompanied by two hundred genuflections; the second to the recitation of the fifty last psalms, but immersed in cold water, holding the heart, the eyes and the hands lifted towards Heaven; the third he devoted to a short rest, lying on the bare stone." Now, these same practices were preserved and practiced by an army of monks, in the episcopal centres which were founded by him or followed his example. These monks devoted themselves to the same prayers: the recitation of the whole office every day, daily prostrations repeated three hundred times, very numerous signs of the cross, baths in icy water and during the recitation of prayers standing up with the arms in the form of a cross—what the Irish called *crosfigill*, " vigil or prayer of the cross ".

Finally, we must place amidst the precious patrimony left to Ireland by her holy apostle, the rallying sign of the three-leaved shamrock. According to tradition, it was in the course of a sermon that remained famous, at Cashel, one of the most sacred religious centres in Ireland, that the saint, to make his hearers understand or at least to explain to them the great mystery of the Holy Trinity, took up a sprig of the trefoil, and thus suggested *one single God in three persons.* His audience were so filled with enthusiasm at this comparison from nature that the trefoil became the symbol of the Catholic faith and the badge of Irish patriotism—and so it has remained ever since. May we conclude with Dom Gougand: *For having annexed Ireland to the kingdom of God, amid so many sufferings and tribulations, with unrivalled Christian heroism, his people have honoured and blessed him throughout the ages, as has been the case with no other national apostle.*

ST. PATRICK'S BREASTPLATE
Translated by J. Ryan, S.J.

I arise to-day
  through a mighty strength, the invocation of the Trinity,
  through belief in the threeness,
  through confession of the oneness
  of the Creator of creation.

I arise to-day
> through the strength of Christ with His baptism,
> through the strength of His crucifixion with His burial,
> through the strength of His resurrection with His ascension,
> through the strength of His descent for the Judgment of Doom.

I arise to-day
> through the strength of the love of Cherubim,
> in obedience of angels,
> in the service of the archangels,
> in hope of resurrection to meet with reward,
> in prayers of Patriarchs,
> in predictions of Prophets,
> in preachings of Apostles,
> in faiths of Confessors,
> in innocence of holy Virgins,
> in deeds of righteous men.

I arise to-day
> through the strength of heaven:
> light of sun,
> brilliance of moon,
> splendour of fire,
> speed of lightning,
> swiftness of wind,
> depth of sea,
> stability of earth,
> firmness of rock.

I arise to-day
> through God's strength to pilot me:
> God's might to uphold me,
> God's wisdom to guide me,
> God's eye to look before me,
> God's ear to hear me,
> God's word to speak for me,
> God's hand to guard me,
> God's shield to protect me,
> God's host to secure me,
>> against snares of devils,
>> against temptations of vices,
>> against inclinations of nature,
>> against every one who shall wish me ill,
>>> afar and anear,
>>> alone and in a multitude.

I summon to-day all those powers between me (and these evils)
    against every cruel merciless power that may oppose my body
      and soul,
  against incantations of false prophets,
  against black laws of heathenry,
  against false laws of heretics,
  against craft of idolatry,
  against spells of women and smiths and wizards,
  against every knowledge . . . man's body and soul.
  Christ to protect me to-day
    against poison, against burning,
    against drowning, against wounding,
  so that there may come to me abundance of reward.
  Christ with me, Christ before me, Christ behind me,
  Christ in me, Christ beneath me, Christ above me,
  Christ on my right, Christ on my left.
  Christ in breadth, Christ in length, Christ in height.
  Christ in the heart of every man who thinks of me,
  Christ in the mouth of everyone who speaks of me,
  Christ in every eye that sees me,
  Christ in every ear that hears me.

I arise to-day
  through a mighty strength, the invocation of the Trinity,
  through belief in the threeness,
  through confession of the oneness,
  of the Creator of creation.

PATRICK'S HYMN

Patrick made this hymn. It was made in the time of Laoghaire son of Niall. The cause of its composition, however, was to protect him and his monks against deadly enemies that lay in wait for the clerics. And this is a corslet of faith for the protection of body and soul against devils and men and vices. When anyone shall repeat it every day with diligent intentness on God, devils shall not dare to face him, it shall be a protection to him against every poison and envy, it shall be a defence to him against sudden death, it shall be a corslet to his soul after his death. Patrick sang this when the ambuscades were laid against his coming by Loegaire, that he might not go to Tara to sow the faith. And when it appeared before those lying in ambush that they (Patrick and his monks) were wild deer with a fawn (Benén) following them. And its name is ' Deer's Cry '.

The Monasteries of Ireland, Nurseries of Saints

By GEORGES CERBELAUD-SALAGNAC

WE know what a magnificent impetus Irish monasticism was to receive in the VIth and VIIth centuries, and all the authors who have written about the religious history of Ireland have asked themselves more or less whether the origins should be ascribed to St. Patrick, himself a monk. His stay at the monastery of Saint Honoratus at Lérins, then his long term at Auxerre, near to the monastery that Saint Germanus had founded on the other side of the Yonne, make this question intelligible. Nowadays we may consider that this little problem has been settled and for our part we shall adopt the conclusion of Father John Ryan, S.J.: " Saint Patrick had a certain formation as a monk, but it was as a cleric, not as a monk, that he started his apostolic work among the Irish."

Nevertheless, we must go back to the first bishop of Ireland to find the beginnings of Irish monachism, for it was indeed he who created the first monasteries, of women as well as men. The "church" of Airne is specially quoted (barony of Costello, in the county of Mayo), which was in the hands of an *Abbot*. Other communities were also founded by Patrick at Ath-broon (Meath) and at Senella-Cella-Dumiche (Sligo); it would seem that they were double, consisting of both men and women. Numerous "native" brothers and sisters, one " foreign " sister and fifteen " foreign " monks are all mentioned in the writings of the age of St. Patrick, as having been installed in different places, without counting " the two *barbarian* monks, Conleng and Ercleng, who were left by Patrick at Moyglass (Roscommon) ". Bishop Assicus had monks who came to drag him from his hermitage in Tirconnell, nowadays known as Donegal, where he had hidden himself for seven years.

We also know that Patrick gave the veil of virgins to Monnine, anyway according to Conchubrau, who wrote the life of the latter. Monnine went first to place herself under the spiritual direction of Saint Ivor at Beg-Eri (Wexford); but several years later, followed by fifty nuns, she left Leinster and established herself at Killeavy, near Newry, in the county of Armagh. It was at the very time when Brigid had just founded Kildare, since Monnine paid a visit in passing to her young imitator who was to become so famous. The story of Monnine does not stop there, since there is attributed to her, after Killeavy, where "the rule was strict", the foundation of at least six other churches in Ireland, seven in Scotland and several others in Great Britain, notably at Calvechif, near to the Trent.

We must specially remember in connection with this distant period the first monastic schools of which the foundation is due to St. Patrick or his contemporaries. Now, when anyone speaks of monastic schools, he clearly speaks of monasteries! The schools are those of Ardagh (Longford), Armagh, Dysart (Louth), Ramoan (Antrim), Saul (Down), Slane (Meath) and Trim (Meath), founded, according to tradition, by Patrick himself, then those of Ardmore (Waterford), by Saint Declan, Beg-Eri (Wexford), by Saint Ivor, Emly (Tipperary), by Saint Ailbe, Elphin (Roscommon), by Saint Assicus (Louth), by Saint Mochta, Nendrum (Down), by Saint Caelan, finally Seir (Offaly), by Saint Ciaran the elder.

Worthy beginnings of the flowering that was to take place in the two following centuries! Unless I am mistaken, it was these schools which were to give Irish monachism its special aspect and above all its incomparable radiance. No doubt, at the hands of these converted filidh[1], who were to form the most striking both of the secular and the regular clergy of Ireland, they would replace the schools of the dethroned druids, and they would form generations of layfolk with the new disciplines, while being careful to preserve the Graeco-Latin basis of traditional education. But they were also to be the seminaries of the young Irish Church; it was from their well-springs of conquering faith that those ardent missionaries, soon to be apostles in the whole of Europe, would draw their refreshment.

Under those conditions there was nothing astonishing in the way the monastic idea spread rapidly across the five provinces of Ireland.[2] All the more so in that it would find favourable soil in these Celtic souls, dreamy and poetic, naturally given to contemplation and to meditation. And it was St. Patrick who set it all going.

We know that at the death of Saint Patrick it was the custom to divide the "holy men" (that is to say those who were living in a holy fashion) into three orders; Bishops, who then numbered 350 according to the Catalogus Sanctorium Hiberniae, monks, 300, and hermits, 100. The "holy men" of the first order, who then were

---

[1] " These latter were poets, and as is always the case with the primitive vates, wizards and thaumaturges and apothecaries as well." Roger Chauviré, History of Ireland.

[2] In our day reduced to four provinces.

3 (A) A symbol of St. Matthew in the Book of Durrow. — 3 (B) Cross of Carndonagh, Co. Donegal.

4 (A) Details of a page of the Gospel Book of Echdernach. — 4 (B) Gospel Book No. 51 in the Library of St. Gall

all bishops, had in their ranks a good number of foreigners; we may believe that they had in fact recognized the pre-eminence of the See of Armagh, and in any case they had a scrupulous respect for the liturgy, the famous Celtic tonsure, and the rule for fixing the date of Easter, established by St. Patrick; finally, they accepted the aid of virgins and of pious women for the service of the sanctuary.

These are the characteristics of the Irish Church at this epoch, and they explain fairly well the development of this Church in the future.

We do not, in reality, think that the distinction between the notion of regular and of secular clergy was, in the mind of Saint Patrick and his contemporaries, as clear as it was to become later on, in Ireland or in other places. While he was a Bishop first of all, did not Patrick more or less combine the episcopal and abbatial functions? The proof is in the fact that at Armagh, Patrick's two first successors, Benen and Jarlath, are called Bishops, but from the time of the next, Cormac, the title of Abbot prevails. Now, we are certain that between Jarlath and Cormac, the Church of Armagh underwent no profound transformation, that the " Abbot " of Armagh continued to be the " Bishop " of the principal See of Ireland. It is in fact the hierarchy which is transformed, as we shall see.

Another thing is brought to light by Dom Louis Gougaud when he writes that " there were no towns in Ireland ". The Irish tribal organization was fundamentally rural. The royal residences (even that of the High King at Tara) were no more than villas scarcely surrounded by a large village, perhaps what we would nowadays call a hamlet. St. Patrick's object was always to instal a bishop alongside each local king. Now, what was more suitable for developing contemplative communities than this tribal organization ?

" When a chief was converted, he agreed to receiving a missionary, besides giving the site for a church, and that for a monastic colony, this to be recruited even from the start from the men of his clan."

If there were 350 bishops in 461, it is obvious that Ireland did not have 350 dioceses! Even admitting that each of the 184 tribes had its bishop, we are still far from the number. Some 150 bishops were thus either itinerants or at the head of communities which were already monastic.

It is not difficult to see that this organization of the primitive Irish Church provided a most suitable ground for the spread of monasticism and one can then better understand the transformation of the hierarchy which took place in the VIth century.

:-:   :-:   :-:

The monastic idea which was sown here and there with Christianity itself, in soil particularly favourable for its development, was not yet sufficient. A wind was still needed to scatter the grain across the earth. This wind blew from the east, from the *Candida Casa,* and also from the British Church.

Twenty years after the arrival of Patrick in Ireland, in the first decade of the Vth century, the British Bishop Ninian, after a pilgrimage to Rome, went to settle among the Picts of Galloway, at Whithorn (nowadays the county of Wigtown, Scotland). Turning away from wood, the normal material, he used white stone for building his church, whence the name *Candida Casa,* when referring to the monastery.

A hundred years later the *Candida Casa,* which had merited the epithet of *Magnum Monasterium,* had become a school of note, a true "noviciate of the spiritual life", which counted among its pupils Enda, Tigernach, Eogan, Finnian, Coirpre. These were famous Irishmen, who were to become ardent propagators of Irish monachism.

We will admit that it was Enda who, the first in Ireland, introduced monasticism of strict observance, with vows, withdrawal from the world and severe discipline. He built his establishment on the island of Aran, off the coast of Galway, facing the Atlantic. In his turn, and very rapidly, he formed disciples who were named Ciaran the Younger, Finnian (already seen at the *Candida Casa*) and Jarlath.

Eogan settled at Ardstraw (in the County Tyrone), Coirpre at Coleraine (County Derry), north of Dál-nAraide and Tigernach at Clones (County Monaghan). Their first recruits, all on fire with youthful ardour, were to be the filijd taught in the monastic schools already planted on Irish soil.

As for the British Church, herself young and conquering, it is not surprising that she also had an influence on her Irish sister. They owed it to each other, for the Celtic peoples, having become the apostles of Christianity, needed to stand together in reciprocal communion of interests.

Saint Cadoc, of Lancarvan, remained for three years at Lismore, and Cybi, another Welshman, spent four years on the Aran islands. Saint Samson himself went to Ireland, "with some highly educated Scots who had come back from Rome", also Saint Gildas. As for the great Saint David, of Myuyv, he was surely "the foreign master most sought after by Irish monks". On their side, Irish monks stayed in the monasteries of Wales and Armorica; others retired into hermitages, while others founded yet further monasteries, such as Sezi who appears to have left Ireland with seventy of his disciples. His monastery gave birth to the little town of Guissény.

Among the disciples of David at Myuyv we find Aidan (also called Maedoc), Scolan and Modomnoc. It is also known that Finnian of

Clonard, Senan, Finnbar and Brendan of Clonfert visited Saint David's monastery.

Between Ireland and Armorica, by Scotland and Wales, there was thus established a regular current of monastic ideals. Now Armorica was Gaul, a doorway open wide to all the influences which had come from what had been the Roman Empire.

Some years after Saint Enda had established himself on Aran, a pure and brilliant star arose in the firmament of the Irish Church. We have already referred to Brigid, who, about 487, founded Kildare. Of noble family, of the Fotharta in Offaly, she was naturally destined by her father to marry and found a home. As she held different opinions, she preferred to leave her father's house and took refuge with Macaille, " the most holy bishop of happy memory " who complied with her desire. At the foot of the altar Brigid vowed her virginity to the Lord and received the veil and the white robe of consecrated virgins. Numerous disciples, as many men as women, came to her, when they heard of her fame, and she found herself led to establish for them the great monastery on the plains of the Liffey. It was in fact, then, a double monastery, where the sisters took their place under the shepherd's crook of the Abbess, and the brothers under that of the Bishop-Abbot. But, as far as we can know from her *Vita,* the work of Cogitose, Kildare must have been like the communities established by Saint Patrick rather than the monasteries of rigorous discipline of the type which Enda had created in Ireland, and which were going to receive their full flowering with Finnian of Clonard.

There were, however, four or five monasteries about which we must say a few words, which were founded before Clonard : Cluainfois and Tuam, Dromore and Monasterboice, whose foundations go back to around the year 500.

Cluainfois (Galway) was the work of Jarlath who either a little earlier, at the same time or a little later, founded not far from there Tuam (Galway). Járlath would have been dead in 545. That is almost all we know of him. His disciple Colman Mac Leiniu founded in his turn the monastery of Cloyne in the south of the County Cork.

Dromore (Down) is connected with the name of Saint Colman, who is still called Mocholmocc, and who must not be confused with the previous one. Finally, Saint Buithe is clearly the founder of Monasterboice in the country of Brega (Louth), since it bears his own name; Monaster Boice is merely a distortion of Mainistir Buithe, which means the monastery of Buithe. This holy man was a bishop and he belonged to the people called Cianachta in Brega; 521 is given as the year of his death.

:-:   :-:   :-:

And now we have reached the threshold of the great period of Irish monachism of which the founder of Clonard can, to a large extent, be considered the father. Everything we have said up to now is merely an introduction. Everything which was done on the soil of the ancient Hibernia, between 432, when Patrick set foot on the small island which always bears his name, Inis Padraig, and 520, is only in fact a providential preparation for the missionary vocation of Ireland.

In fact, apart from Saint Patrick, the greatest Irish saints were monks, and monks who moved, who left their original monasteries and their country in order to throng in large numbers abroad. Patrick's special mission was to convert a people, and, aided by the grace of God, he succeeded in this beyond all his hopes. But God would require more from this people. A century had not passed when He was taking the best of His sons between His hands to make them in their turn astonishing instruments for the propagation of the faith.

One may say that the second part of the religious history of Ireland begins quite definitely with the foundation of Clonard in 520.

It was then that the ordinary hierarchy established by Saint Patrick became a monastic hierarchy. Jurisdiction passed into the hands of Bishop-Abbots and Priest-Abbots who ruled their parishes from their monasteries. There were also bishops without monastic vows (like other clerics), but they did not constitute the national hierarchy, which was in every way responsible for the ecclesiastical government of the country. As regards this question of the relations between the monks and the ecclesiastical authorities in Ireland during the VIth century, Father John Ryan does not hesitate to say that the monks themselves were the ecclesiastical authorities. The few bishops who were not monks and their bishoprics were from then on of negligible importance.

This triumph of the monastic ideal was not one of the least original qualities of the Irish Church.

:-:   :-:   :-:

For a long time the monastery of Saint Finnian, amidst the peaceful pastures of Erard (Cluain-Iraird, in the county of Meath) was to be the most attractive spiritual home of the five provinces. It is said that the eminent Abbot had as many as three thousand disciples round him; maybe we need see no more in this vast figure than a way of meaning a great number; or even a hagiographical desire to equal Finnian with Pachomius, who also, according to the testimony of Palladius, had three thousand monks in his monastery in the Thebaïd! However that may be, Finnian was a master in the full sense of the word, and he formed many disciples. People came to him not only out of a desire for a more perfect life but also in order to learn. His great claim to glory, that to which hagiographers have paid special attention, is that of having taught those who are called the " twelve apostles of Ireland ", that is to say Ciaran the elder, Ciaran the younger, Columcille, Brendan of Clonfert, Brendan of Birr, Colman of Terryglass, Molaisse, Canice, Ruadan, Mobí, Sinnel and Nannid.

But we can see at once how there is something artificial about such a list, since Ciaran the elder had already figured among the five " pre-Patricians " . . . ! If he was, perhaps not a pre-Patrician, at least the contemporary of St. Patrick, as it seems we must admit, it is clearly impossible to find him among the disciples of Saint Finnian three-quarters of a century later. In order to safeguard the figure twelve, which is eminently sacred, we can always replace Saint Ciaran the elder by Finnian himself! Thus everyone will be content, and historical probability will lose nothing.

In any case, these eleven principal disciples whose authenticity we have no reason to suspect, in their turn founded monasteries with schools which were soon as celebrated as that of Clonard. Thus, through them, the spirit, the rule, the discipline, the teaching of Clonard, the product of Saint Finnian's powerful personality, the young Church in Ireland, all bubbling over with the zeal of neophytes, was to receive a fresh impulse.

Ciaran the younger was the son of a Meath carpenter who had emigrated to Connaught where taxation was less heavy. The carpenters, who were at the same time coach-builders and wheelwrights, formed part of what might be called the well-off bourgeoisie, and Ciaran's father was regarded as a relatively rich man. The young student was first of all one of Enda's monks, in the monastery of Aran, beaten about by all the ocean winds. He ended by letting his soul be moulded by Finnian's irresistible persuasion. Finally, about 548, on the left bank of the Shannon, to the South of Lough Ree, " on the edge of the province of Connaught ", he founded the great monastery of Clonmacnoise (Offaly). The founder did not however long enjoy his position as a master; he died the following year. Perhaps he was not yet thirty-five years old. Nevertheless, he was already famous and it is said that the influence of Clonmacnoise reached over half of Ireland.

Columcille came of a very noble line. By his father he was descended from Niall of the Nine Hostages (whose line provided the High Kings for more than five centuries), and by his mother from the hero Cathair Mor, founder of the great line of the Kings of Leinster. When he came into the world, it was his uncle Muirchertach Mac Erc who was reigning at Tara. He himself could have claimed the highest dignities, but he preferred the service of God alone and fled to Clonard, where he received minor orders, then the priesthood. Did he do a term in the company of Comgall, Ciaran and Canice at Glasnevin, the monastery of Saint Mobí ? This is of little importance. In 546, flying on his own wings, he established his first foundation at Derry, in the north of Ulster. We say his "first" foundation, for the cousin of the High King could not be content with one single house for his God; Columcille was a builder. Ten years after Derry, Durrow rose from the ground, in the principality of Fir-Ceall, in the midlands. Then there was Kells, at the north-west of Meath, which was only to become of real importance at the beginning of the IXth century, when the monks of Iona, fleeing from the Norsemen, came there seeking for refuge. Swords (Dublin), Drumcliff (Sligo), Tory Island (Donegal) also owed their existence to the activities of Columcille. But his great title to glory is to be sought outside Ireland, in the little island of Iona which is Scottish territory, and forms part of the county of Argyll. Iona, however, belongs unquestionably to Irish religious history. Founded by an Irishman, inhabited by Irishmen, Iona was always an Irish community, in fact a threshold built by the missionaries from Ireland that they might be the better able to set out for the conquest of the world.

There are two Brendans among Finnian's disciples; the one founded Birr, the other Clonfert. Certainly the latter is much better known than the former. Little is known of Brendan of Birr, except that he made a foundation, probably about 560, in the county of Offaly on the Little Brosna, a tributary of the Shannon. On the other hand his namesake is perhaps the most popular saint in Ireland for he is known as the Navigator! But before setting out to sea, he stayed with his friend Columcille at Iona and founded Clonfert in 557 on the eastern side of Connaught.

Colman, the son of Crimthann, before dying of the plague in 549, had time to found the monastery of Terryglass in Co. Tipperary. The reputation which this house held for holiness and learning was soon such that Columcille did not fail to visit it during one of his stays in Ireland; it was also perhaps on account of the friendship which bound the founder of Iona to that of Terryglass.

Molaisse, who is also called Laisreu, settled about 530 on an island of Loch Erne, Devenish (Fermanagh); he died about 564. It would seem that he should also be regarded as the father of a monastery of secondary importance, situated on the island of Murray, on the Sligo coast.

Canice, an intimate friend of Columcille's, started by evangelizing Scotland and the islands which are strewn along the west coast of that country. On his return to his own country, he travelled south-wards and ended by founding a church and a monastery at Aghaboe, in Upper Ossory (Co. Kilkenny). It was there that he breathed his last in the year 600.

As for the four last " apostles " of Ireland, they are known above all by their foundations: Ruadan at Lorrha in Ormond (Tipperary); Mobí at Glasnevin (Dublin); Sinnel at Cleenich (Fermanagh); Nannid at Inismacsaint on Lough Erne (Fermanagh).

Finally, the following foundations are also attributed to monks from Clonard, disciples of Finnian: Kilglin, in the south of Brega, by Mogennoc; Achonry, by Nathi; Inishkeen in Louth, near Monaghan, by Daig; Killeigh, in Offaly, by Sinchell; Moynarney and New Ross in Wexford, by Abbau Mac Cormaic; Kinnity, barony of Bally-brit in Offaly, by Fínán Camm; Latteragh, barony of Upper Ormond in Tipperary, by Saint Odian, who died in 549; Clonfod, in the parish of Killucan in Meath, by Saint Etchenn; Monadrehid, near Borris-in-Ossory, by a Saint Laisren who would not be the same as the Molaisse of Devenish; Russagh, near Killabon in Meath, by Saint Caeman Brec.

By Clonard, and by these direct filiations one can tell the influence of Saint Finnian. This influence did not stop there: we find it again, in a more indirect manner, it is true, but nevertheless very real, down to the end of the great monastic period. The pupils of Finnian, having become masters, then founded monastic schools, of which the pupils in their turn became founders; this went on for five or six generations. And, finally, perhaps everything flowed from Clonard.

Can one risk a chronological account of the great monasteries of the VIth and VIIth centuries which were founded by monks other than the direct disciples of Saint Finnian ? Certainly, at least of the principal ones among them, and with certain necessary reserves. It will be understood that the dates put forward by the *Vitae* having to be accepted with caution; it is necessary to accept without too much discussion those laid down by tradition. Here then is an attempt at classification, especially following the picture supplied by Hugh Graham, completed by the lists of Father John Ryan.

In 537, Saint Senan settled in the island of Scattery, at the mouth of the Shannon (Clare), and in 548, Saint Fintan settled at Clonenagh, in the principality of Laoigis. The latter, who was a disciple of Colman of Terryglass, soon surpassed his master and all the other solitaries of the period by the austerity of his life. We must believe that the Irish had by then achieved a sufficient degree of mystical maturity, for, according to the author of the *Vita*, tonsured men came to him from all sides. " They worked with their hands, in the manner of the hermits, cultivating the ground with a simple hoe. They refused to employ any animal, even a cow. If they were offered a little milk or some butter, they declined the offer with thanks. If anyone was by chance to introduce some milk into the house unbeknown to the severe Abbot, the latter would have the jug containing it broken, as soon as he discovered it. Wild herbs and green vegetables formed the only daily fare of the community, just as water was their only drink." If one may believe the martyrology of OEugus, Fintan submitted himself to even greater mortifications than those imposed on his companions. " The generous Fintan never took anything else during his life except dried barley bread and muddy water." Being rightly moved by these austerities, the monks of the neighbourhood came to the conclusion that the rigour of Fintan's rule was excessive. Led by Canice of Aghaboe they came to Clonenagh to reprimand the Abbot. Being warned by an angel, Fintan welcomed his critics with much kindness, granted a measure of flour to each of his monks to do honour to their visit, regaled them with edifying conversation, and as soon as they were gone put his community back on the usual régime of vegetables and muddy water. He died in 603.

In 551 we find Saint Nessan at Mungret, not far from Limerick. Four years after, however, Moville, and another four years later, Bangor, will have more claim on our attention. They were in fact two of the most important monasteries in Ireland, and the fame of the founder of the first is scarcely inferior to that of the founder of the second. As for the latter, it may be enough to say that he was the master of St. Columban!

Finnian of Moville came from the Dal-Fiatach, the royal people of Ulster, and the day came when he was called to be the chief. Apart from Moville, Finnian raised a monastery at Dromin, in Co. Louth. It has been claimed that he introduced the " law " of Moses into Ireland, so may we perhaps conclude that the " Gospels " which Columcille copied without Finnian's permission, who was their proprietor, were really the Old Testament ?

Finnian died in 579 and his monastery for some years to come continued to be the most flourishing in the country, but Bangor, which was not many miles away, would not be long in supplanting it.

Comgall was a Pict who belonged to the colony founded by that people on the coast of Ulster. He was born in 517 and settled in 559 (others say in 555, but the former date seems to be the best attested) in the Ards of Ulster, on the southern side of Belfast Lough, at Bangor, which is nowadays a town of twenty thousand inhabitants.

Closely connected with Columcille, he then visited Scotland, where he left a visible mark of his presence there, the monastery of the " Land of Heth ", the island of Tiree in the county of Argyll. He died in 603. Comgall is one of the great saints of the Irish Church;

thus, and as such, does he figure in the litanies of the Stowe Missal. In the Bangor Antiphonary, compiled in the monastery between the years 680 and 691, we find a hymn in his honour and a panegyric of his rule. Bangor was a centre of high Christian spirituality till the time of the Danish invasions, and Saint Bernard, in the XIIth century, in his *Life of Saint Malachy,* did not hesitate to call it " an eminently sacred place, the nursery of saints which has produced so many abundant fruits for the glory of God." Has it not been said that one member of the congregation of Bangor himself founded a hundred monasteries ? If some of his brethren were able to imitate him up to a point, of how many foundations was Bangor not the mother-house ?

There are also, belonging to the sixth century, but without it being possible to be more definite about them, foundations made by other monks who are more or less known to us in other ways. There is Aedh who seems to have been very well known in his lifetime. He belonged to the family of the Southern Uí Néill, and he chose for his chief foundation Killair, near to the hill of Uisneach, in the county of Westmeath. If, however, one may trust the hagiography of the period, he was also active in Connaught, Munster and Leinster. He was probably a bishop and he died in 589. The radiance of Killair, like that of Aedh's other foundations, Enach-Briuin, in Ormond, and Rath-Aedha (Westmeath), scarcely survived the death of the saint.

Molua, or Lugaid, passes for a disciple of Comgall of Bangor and Finnian of Clonard, which is very doubtful as regards the latter, for at the death of Finnian, Molua was probably no more than a child, if indeed he had yet been born! Never mind—he founded a " great and famous " monastery on the borders of Munster and Leinster, on land which was given by Berach, the King of Laoigis. This monastery even bore the name of the founder, Clonfertmulloc. Other churches are credited to Molua, Slievebloom and Drumsnatt (Monaghan); his proverbial tenderness towards all beings endowed with life, whether human or animal, is praised. It is remembered that on a certain day in 608 all the birds suddenly began to lament. An angel brought the explanation of this to Mael Anfaid, the Abbot of Lismore, who was astonished at the phenomenon : " It is because, oh cleric, Molua, who never killed the smallest bird, has just died!"

Why did Colman Mac Beogna, who probably came from the Southern Uí Néill, give to the monastery which he founded at Fid-Elo the name of Lann-Elo ? There has been well founded astonishment over this, for there is nothing in Colman's life that shows any possible Breton influence. He was ordained priest at some place which is not quite clear, but certainly in Ireland, he settled for a time at Connor in Antrim, then went on several journeys to Scotland, and finally settled in Meath, less than seven kilometres from Durrow. Now *lann* is undeniably a Breton word, which would have originally meant land surrounded by an enclosure, then a monastery and a church. In Wales and in Armorica it is to be found in a great number of place-names, but in modern Breton it simply means *lande* (heath). Colman was well known as a man of learning; to him is attributed the drafting of the little work known as *The Alphabet of Devotion*. Did he sin from pride or was he just a little too proud of his intellectual achievements ? We are always told that, as a punishment, God suddenly deprived him of his memory. He only recovered it thanks to the fraternal intervention of Molua, his contemporary and friend. Colman died at Lann-Elo in 611, at the age of fifty-six years.

> He was the soldier of Christ in the country of Ireland,
> And his name is famous even beyond the seas;
> Kevin the Virtuous, the warrior with the fair hair,
> At the end of the valley between the two great lakes.

Thus does the oldest Irish calendar sing of Saint Kevin in a quatrain, in the style of the heroes of old! The two lakes are at Glendalough, " the valley of the two lakes ", where Kevin in fact founded a monastery which became one of the best known in Ireland. It is easy to understand how this man of Leinster, the lover of solitude, should have chosen this enchanting but retired site, this spot of mountains and woodland, where there is water in abundance, mysterious lakes and foaming streams. The number of monks grouped round Kevin was soon so great that new buidings were needed and cells. But Kevin, rather than this crowd, preferred a retreat which he had made for himself, " where the trees grew in close ranks and where the streams flowed clear ". He lived there as a hermit in a rough hut, spending as much as four years on end there without fire or roof. It is said that the wild animals showed him their friendship and came to drink in familiar fashion from the hollow of his hand. Kevin died in 618 at a very advanced age.

To the same period clearly belong Fachtna, the founder of Roscarbery (Cork), and Comman, whose name is connected with Roscommon, Colm, who founded the monastery of Inis Celtra or Holy Island on Lough Derg, near Killaloe, and Bairre, that of Cork. Finally, Macartan, the founder of Clogher (Tyrone), and another Canice, the founder of Kilkenny.

To finish with this rich flowering of monasteries of men, it only remains for us to mention the two important foundations of the VIIth century, Lismore (Waterford), in 635, due to Saint Carthach, and Mayo, in 665, due to another Saint Colman.

And what about the women ? We have already evoked the grand figure of Saint Brigid of Kildare after that of Saint Monnine. In the following generations, several virgins would follow in their steps, and deserve a special mention. First of all clearly comes St. Ita, who belonged to the famous people of the Deisi. With much trouble (and, so it is said, thanks to the intervention of an angel) she was able to overcome the resistance of her parents, receive the veil of virginity, and exile herself to the green pasture-lands of Killeedy, at the foot of Sliabh Luachra, in what is now Co. Limerick. Virgins came to her from all the neighbouring districts, to follow her teaching which could be summed up in these three points, a true faith in God in purity of heart, simplicity of life in religion, and generosity in charity. She founded a school for little boys and had among her pupils some future saints, such as Brendan of Clonfert who spent five years of his young days at Killeedy. Our Abbess also won for herself the name of "foster-mother of the saints of Ireland". Ita, before dying, between the years 570 and 577, predicted that her monastery of women would transform itself one day into a monastery of men, which indeed took place some hundred years later.

There was another monastery of women which had an assured reputation; it was that which Saint Cairech Dergan founded in the county of Roscommon. Nothing is known of the foundress except a genealogy to be accepted with caution, and the year of her death, 577 or 578; but her house, for several centuries, had an influence comparable with that of Kildare.

Aghavea (barony of Magherastephana, Fermanagh) and Kell-Rignige (Meath) which are often mentioned as only consisting of simple churches, very likely had monastic origins due respectively to Saint Lasaire and Saint Ricinne.

Finally, during the last years of the VIIth century, we should mention Clainn-Bonaig, in the county of Meath, founded by Saint Samthanne, who died in 739. This monastery was also for a long time a well-known spiritual centre, but with it there really comes to an end what we must call the great period of Irish monachism.

Such a force of radiance and expansion can only be accounted for by a very high spirituality and also a rigorous sanctity. Faithful to the traditional monastic ideal which made a religious a soldier of Christ, the monks of Ireland, in order that they might conquer the better, submitted to an iron discipline.

At the head of the community there was an Abbot, who was invested with absolute government, and who was usually seconded in his administration by a minister or private secretary. Around them the seniors took their places, old-established brothers who had reached a high degree of perfection in the practice of the virtues. They had the charge of directing and correcting the young monks, forming them and preparing the novices.

When an Abbot governed several monasteries, he would relegate his powers, wherever he did not reside, to officers or local superiors.

Later the need made itself felt to name a certain number of officers who would complete the hierarchy. There was thus the Vice-Abbot, often known as the Prior, who seems to have been in early times the bursar or administrator of the material goods of the monastery. The same held true of the cellarer and the guest-master.

After them came the crowd of monks, whether priests or not, among whom was to be found every sort of trade; peasants and masons, weavers, goldsmiths and silversmiths, cooks and labourers, and also men of letters and illuminators. Thus the community was self-sufficient.

The monasteries had little resemblance to those we are accustomed to see in our days. The expression " monastic cities " would be nearer the point for describing them. Each monk, in fact, inhabited a hut in the form of a hive, built of clay and hurdles, a cell built with his own hands; the furniture consisted of a bed of skins, a pillow of stone covered with straw or dry leaves, a bench, a cross cut out of solid wood, without forgetting the reed stuck into tallow instead of a lamp. Special cells were reserved for artists, those who copied and ornamented the books. At times the larger huts sheltered two, three, four or seven monks, or an even larger number. But the Abbot always had a cell for himself alone.

Alongside the church, the only buildings of any importance were the refectory and the guest-house.

Naturally, in the use of the time of the religious prayer held the chief place. To private prayers, in which each was his own master, were added the prayers in common. Five times by day and three times by night the monks assembled in the church for the recitation in common of the canonical hours, prime, terce, sext, none, vespers, compline, nocturnes and matins.

Almost everywhere Mass was only celebrated on Sundays and feast days; sometimes on Saturdays. It thus acquired a special importance. Communion was thus only given on those days. In order to punish grave offences against the rule, the Abbot could forbid access to the Holy Table.

One must read the *Penitential* and the *Rule* of Saint Columban to have an idea of the discipline which ruled in these monasteries. Every fault, however slight, was inexorably sanctioned by a punishment most carefully fixed in advance; corporal punishments were not excluded.

Among these ascetics, penance also took on severe forms, genuflexions renewed by the hundred, interminable prayers, with the arms in the form of a cross, so motionless that the birds came and settled on the extended fingers, if one may believe Marguerite-Marie Dubois, who adds, as regards Saint Columban, " immersions in freezing water; a complete fast for several days; mortifications of every kind ". Columban, in his love of the cross, found his delight in the " good rule " of Bangor, which an old sequence described as " right and divine, strict, holy and exact, supremely just and worthy of admiration, and which belongs to the blessed life which God prepares in the company of the saints, to last without end ". For, in order to mortify the senses and especially carnal desires, the Irish gave themselves with spirit to the most severe practices, of which freezing baths, scourgings and prolonged fasts were among the most ordinary!

Such are the most characteristic feature of Irish monachism; many of these practices came no doubt in a direct line from the Thebaïd and from the school of Saint Pachomius, others are local revivals common to all the centuries, but the monks of Ireland, having adapted them to their customs and their climate, knew how to include them in their own rules of life which confer their originality.

:-:   :-:   :-:

Certainly, all these brilliant stars which were lit for two centuries in the sky of Irish Christianity, were not extinguished all of a sudden when the decadence set in. Their radiance was to make itself felt with more or less intensity in the ages which followed, and certainly outside Ireland rather than in Ireland itself. The interminable quarrels between the O'Connors of Connaught, the Uí Néill of Ailech and the Uí Néill of the Midlands for the possession of the High King's throne, were not of a nature to hinder the development and action of the monasteries; besides, the monks always kept themselves remarkably above temporal rivalries. Nevertheless these feuds had a dangerous and weakening effect on the national strength before a possible external danger. And this danger was suddenly present on all the shores of Ireland in the form of the Danish invaders. They were pagans, brothers of those Normans, who were at the same time ravaging Gaul.

From the seaboard to the East where they had established their first bases, they were not long in invading the north and in reaching the west with their rapid boats. They were seen on Lough Neagh; they devastated Armagh, then moved up the Shannon and sacked

Clonmacnoise. Having installed themselves solidly at the mouths of the rivers, they established important ports, Dublin, Wexford, Waterford, Cork, Limerick. Not being able to drive them back to the sea, the Kings of the provinces and the peoples, grouped at last around the High King, had to reconcile themselves to their presence and to come to terms with them.

A. Rivollan states that in the course of their raids, " the pirates preferred to attack the churches and the monasteries, because precious objects were accumulated there, and also from hatred of Christianity". They struck indeed a terrible blow at Irish monachism from which it did not recover. We can understand thenceforth the lamentations of Saint Malachy and of his biographer Saint Bernard as to the decrepit state, four centuries later, of the Irish Church in general and of the monasteries in particular, and the moral and spiritual degeneracy of the inhabitants of the whole island.

:-:   :-:   :-:

The Irish monastic movement, which was admirable in itself, would have been no more than a purely local phenomenon and of no universal importance if had been confined in its action within the island. This was not the case. On the contrary, the numbers of monks from Ireland, fresh from the great monastic schools, strike us as impetuous apostles, eager to carry the Gospel to the four corners of Europe, and to implant at all the latitudes monasteries submitted to their iron rule! Father White, in his *Apologia*, puts forward the view that Ireland gave 115 missionaries to Germany, 45 to France, 44 to England, 36 to Belgium, 25 to Scotland and 13 to Italy. If one may accept the testimony of Jonas, the biographer of Saint Columban, no less than 620 missionaries had left Luxeuil to swarm over Bavaria alone. Naturally they would not all have been Irish, but a good number among them must surely have been.

We know that Saint Columcille founded a monastery on the Scottish isle of Iona and that this was peopled above all by Irishmen. From Iona the Irish monks not only made for the south, for England and the Continent, but they also spread among the northern islands. Such was Cormac who was the first to carry the Gospel to the wild Picts of the Orkneys. Later in the VIIIth century, some other monks of Iona, according to Dicuil, reached the Shetlands and went as far as the Faroes. Finally, according to this geographer, it was again the monks of Ireland who discovered Iceland about 795, some three-quarters of a century before the date recognized for its discovery by the Scandinavians. Dom Gougaud judiciously remarks on this subject that the testimony of Dicuil is "confirmed by the Icelandic tradition recorded in the Islendingabok and the Landnamabok ".

Let us mention here only for memory's sake the name of Saint Brendan the navigator, and then let us return to Iona and to Columcille. The country known nowadays under the name of Scotland, and which was the home of the Scots and the Picts, was almost entirely evangelized by the Irish missionary monks. Even the Picts of the South, who had formerly been converted by Saint Ninian, the founder of the *Candida Casa,* and who had reverted to paganism, owe to them their second conversion, and this thanks to the 32 monasteries established among the Scots and to the 21 monasteries established among the Picts by Columcille or at his instigation.

However, the victorious pagan princes had ruined Christianity in England. From the time of his arrival, Oswald, who had been exiled among the Scots and baptized by the monks of Iona, had at heart the restoration of Christianity in his territory. He naturally applied to his own masters in religion. The Abbot of Iona lost no time in complying with his desire and chose the Irishman Aidan who was forthwith consecrated bishop. Aidan fixed his choice on a small island of the North Sea, Lindisfarne, facing the royal residence of Bamburgh (nowadays Holy Island in Northumberland).

Lindisfarne, the daughter of Iona, marks a fresh leap ahead in that completely spiritual conquest of Europe by the Irish. Dom Gougaud says of Aidan's monastery that it "was the most powerful home of religious influence in England ". When Aidan died in 651, another Irishman, Finan, succeeded him. Lindisfarne in its turn swarmed across England. There are usually placed to its credit the foundations of Coldingham, Mailros and Lastingham in Northumbria, Ripon and Whitby in Yorkshire, Burgh Castle in Suffolk, Saint Bees in Lancashire, Malmesbury, founded by Maeldub, among the Saxons of the West (Wessex), Bosham, founded by Dicuil, in Sussex, and Glastonbury " of the Gaels " in Somerset.

At all times the Irish were to be found on the Continent, they remained there, they were monks, priests and hermits, and we know that when Saint Patrick arrived at Auxerre he found there an Irishman among Saint Amateur's clerics. The development of Irish monachism and the desire for the apostolate which resulted from it, could not fail to incite the sons of green Erin to take the road to those countries where the barbarian hordes were spreading abroad the virus of all the heresies. If the story of Gibrieu, of his six brothers, Trésain, Hélain, Germain, Véran, Abran and Pétran, and of the three sisters, Franche, Promptie and Porcie, who would have come in 508 into the region of Chalons-sur-Marne in order to evangelize it, should only be accepted with caution, nevertheless it is inspired by real facts, perhaps many of them, of which it would then be a synthesis. In any case, with or without brothers and sisters, Gibrien on the one hand and Trésain on the other, certainly existed. The relics of the former were venerated at Rheims; they were profaned and dispersed, like so many others, at the Revolution.

Still in the VIth century Fridolin entered France, he stayed for a long time at Poitiers where he became Abbot, then, having taken up his pilgrim's staff, he travelled to Lorraine, Alsace, Burgundy, Switzerland, evangelizing, baptizing, establishing churches. He ended by settling at Seckingen, not far from Basel, where he founded a double monastery in honour of Saint Hilarius.

It is said that Frigdien, or Frediano, who died as Bishop of Lucca in Tuscany, about 588, was none other than Finnian of Moville. But the apostolic work of the Irish on the Continent is dominated, and from a height, by the name of Saint Columban, that giant whose prestige and renown would be sufficient to throw all the others into the shade. A nobleman of Leinster, he did not pass through Iona, but through Cleenich and Bangor, where he was formed in the rough school of Comgall. He thus came directly from Ireland to Gaul, only passing through Great Britain in transit.

It was by him, by his disciples and those who carried on his work, the unwearying builders of monasteries, that Gaul, then Germany and Italy were to know a monastic revival by which they were and remained profoundly affected.

5 Tara Brooch in the Dublin Museum.

A   B

6 (A) The pillar of Crayant (Indre-et-Loire)   6 (B) The cross of Ahenny, Co. Tipperary

Irishmen in Peril on the Sea

By RENÉ P. MILLET

IRELAND was, of all the countries of the Western world, the one which, in the course of the Middle Ages, showed the greatest originality. This island, which never saw a Roman legionary on its soil, which was the first non-Romanized country to receive the faith of Christ, which did not know the smallest martyrdom, saw a Church arise gifted with a highly attractive personality. The singularities of her liturgy, such as her method for calculating the date of Easter, the crescent-shaped tonsure worn by the monks, the identification of the church with the monastery—or, to be more exact, the religious centre of the group of hermits which is usually designated by that name—caused the Irish to be treated as heretics. These peculiar monks gave themselves up to strange mortifications in their "monasteries": prolonged prayers, adoration on their knees with their arms in the form of a cross, scourgings, baths in icy water, complete seclusion, etc. . . . Certain of them made surprising vows, such as to give themselves up to the peril of the waves in unsafe ships, sometimes without oars and only furnished with a rudimentary sail; they made the resolution not to return to their own country for a considerable time—sometimes until death—and to leave it to God to lead them wherever He willed. The innumerable lives of Irish saints often speak of these "voyages for the love of God (or of Christ)", of these "journeyings in order to discover the heavenly country".

What was it that pushed these monks on to fulfil such vows?

In its origins, in the spirit of St. Pachomius or St. Antony, the hermit life was a retreat to the desert, in the manner of Saint John the Baptist. In Ireland, there was no desert, but there were men who wished to live in solitude, far from contact with other human beings, who retired into remote places which were difficult of access; these were their "deserts": retired valleys, stony hills, the hollow places of the coast. Often the renown of the holy man surpassed the hostility of the countryside; disciples flowed in and set up their cells around him who had known so well how to show them the way of renunciation, and whom with one accord they chose as their leader, their Abbot. Often, in order to protect this assembly of huts from the outer world, they built a wall, so that the whole formed a kind of phalanstery, in which the number of cells could be considerable.

49

Does not the *Life of Saint Brendan* tell us that this monk, the founder of one of the most famous monasteries, Clonfert, before long found himself at the head of three thousand anchorites ?

Certain ascetics could not be content with such a communal life, severe as it was. This it was which led them to seek for " a desert on the ocean ", pushed on as they were by an imperious desire for total solitude. Some of them settled on islands, even on the minute islands along the coast of Ireland; then, crossing the sea they peopled in the same fashion the archipelagoes on the coast of Scotland. Others even went much further, such as Cormac úa Liatháin, who reached the Orkneys, found them inhabited and preached the Gospel to the inhabitants for the first time. But, without exception, the most celebrated of these navigators was St. Brendan about whom not long since they still told stories of an evening in the cottages of Brittany. His history was already known by the monk Raoul Glaber, the chronicler of the year one thousand, just as all Western Europe right up to the shores of the Baltic knew it[1]. Story-tellers and troubadours propagated it, adding episodes, embellishing the initial theme, giving proof of an unbridled imagination, and coming in for the reprobation of numbers of French and German scholars. This is how one could sum up the chief incidents in this legendary account: —

" Having one day heard a monk who was speaking of the existence beyond the sea of a 'Promised Land' inhabited by the saints, Brendan resolved to leave his monastery and go in search of this land. Having made a retreat on a mountain and fasted for forty days, he undertook the building of a ship. When this was finished, he embarked with seventeen companions and began his navigation. He came across many islands, some of them deserted, some of them populated, where he always received kindly hospitality. One day, so we are told, these bold navigators of God came across a tower which rose from the sea to beyond the clouds; it was surrounded by a pavilion with openings, the openings of which were so broad that the ship could pass through sideways. This pavilion was of a glistening white like silver, and had the hardness of marble; the tower was of the purest crystal; the sea seemed to be of the same crystal, it was so clear and transparent. On another day the good monks came across an island inhabited by fierce blacksmiths; it was quite luminous with heat, and surrounded with a boiling sea; it was the entrance of Hell and Saint Brendan lost two companions. At last, the Irishmen found the famous 'Promised Land of the Saints' where they were able to collect quantities of exquisite fruits and precious stones before a

---

[1] The church at Güstrow (Mecklenburg-Schwerin) has frescoes telling of various episodes in the legendary life of St. Brendan.

happy voyage took them back to their monastery. Their journey lasted seven years."

It is an attractive legend.

But what part of this legend can one accept as true, or at least as probable ? In order to reply to this question we must on the one hand analyse the legend in itself and inquire into the sources; on the other hand we must confront it with what we know *historically* of the life of St. Brendan.

As regards the first point, scholars have established that this search for the " Promised Land of the Saints " was derived from the old Celtic legends that the Druids used to tell, who spoke of an Eden situated beyond the seas, a long way to the West. They have proved that the legend is later than the death of St. Brendan, which took place about the year 580; the first known edition is not before the beginning of the IXth century, and its full flowering dates from the XIth and XIIth centuries.

As for the second point, we must make a highly important pre- liminary remark: a number of lives of saints of the early Middle Ages can only be accepted with caution, for they are full of traditional episodes which one keeps finding from one life to the other; and as historical documents, many of them have no more value than the " Song of Roland " as a source for the history of Charlemagne. We have several biographies of St. Brendan, and this is how one could tell his " truthful " history, allowing for all reserves, as we have just said: —

He would have been born at the end of the Vth century, in the south-west of Ireland, in the region of Tralee bay, in what is now Co. Kerry. His parents were rich landed proprietors who had already been converted to Christianity, and they had as director of their consciences a holy bishop of great reputation, called Earc. The birth of Brendan had been accompanied by a miraculous illumination in the night sky, and Saint Earc, when he baptized the child, had foretold a great destiny for him. When he reached the age of ten years, the holy bishop took him into his house where he astonished everyone by his seriousness and his devotion; he spent his spare time in reading sacred works and refused all games. On this subject there is a charming anecdote: one day the daughter of the local king, who also was ten years old, met the young boy in whom she saw an ideal playmate; but he repelled her brutally. The holy bishop, afraid of the possible consequences which such an affront might bring, as a penance put the delinquent in a grotto, with orders that he was not to come out till he himself brought the punishment to an end. At night-time Earc, who was all indulgence, went to the grotto carrying the little boy's meal; on the threshold he fell on his knees; Brendan, surrounded with a supernatural light, was talking to angels who had come to bear him company and to comfort him in his solitude.

Having reached the canonical age, Brendan was ordained to the priesthood, and left his protector. Like many of his compatriots, he chose the monastic life. He set out in quest of a " desert " which he found in the heart of the country near the banks of the Shannon. Soon, guided by his fame, numerous disciples came to set up their cells around his. Thus was founded one of the most brilliant monasteries in Ireland, Clonfert (about 553), which soon had three thousand monks. Brendan, however, left this flourishing community in search of solitude and it was then that he undertook his famous navigation. His first attempt met with a reverse but, quite undiscouraged, he set out anew, seeking for a " secret land ". After a journey lasting two years he returned to his monastery at Clonfert and died there between 577 and 583, aged more than ninety years.

It is onto this stock, which is attested by his biographers, that the fabulous details of the fairy legend which we summarized afore were grafted. The " account of the journey " or *Immram* is furthermore a classical form of the old Celtic legends, and St. Brendan can thus be considered as the Christian hero of a popular traditional type.

But what can have been this mysterious land for which our saint was seeking? The Celtic " paradise " which the bards placed far away to the West, or some deserted island where he could live alone according to his secret vow ? Now, the fact that he returned to his monastery does not seem to confirm this last hypothesis. Was he not then merely looking for new lands to conquer for Christ ? In that case, what countries can he have visited on his travels ? One of his biographers says definitely that he paid a visit to Saint Gildas " in Britain ", that is to say probably in what is now Wales, where he founded numerous monasteries. On the other hand, Adamnan (an Irish monk of the IXth century), the biographer of Saint Columba, the founder of the monastery on Iona, assures us that the latter, having retired to the island of Hinba, received a visit from Brendan of Clonfert, accompanied by Comgall of Bangor, Caimmech d' Achad-bó, and Cormac úa Liatháin. One can judge from these brief statements that Brendan probably visited the coasts and islands of the Irish Sea.

Nevertheless, it is not impossible that St. Brendan and his companions went much further North and that they reached the Orkneys, the Hebrides and the Shetlands. Certain others have even put forward the hypothesis that the fact of placing a " paradise " beyond the sea to the West would prove nothing less than that the Irish knew of America and that St. Brendan discovered it a thousand years before Columbus. This really gives too much rein to the imagination!

Yet there are in the legend two details which deserve to be dwelt on for a moment. There is first the episode of the tower of marble and crystal rising from the sea; and then that of the island with the diabolical blacksmiths belching out fire and surrounded by a boiling sea. It is easy to recognize two natural phenomena well known by geographers, pack-ice and the volcano, phenomena which one finds associated in Iceland. The question which now arises is this: did St. Brendan pursue his voyage till they reached the great island of the North ? Was he in some ways connected with the origins of Christianity in that country?

The Irish did in fact know Iceland. It was a "Scottish" monk of the IXth century, who lived at the court of Louis the Pious, who vouches for this. One can indeed read in the work of Dicuil, *De mensura orbis terrae,* written about 825, that monks from Ireland were occupying, in the course of the VIIth and VIIIth centuries, hermitages in the Faroe Islands beyond the *Ultima Thule* of former times[2]. He also writes that his compatriots discovered Iceland about 795, which would be about sixty-five years before the arrival of the Vikings in that island. Would it not be a manifestation of national pride if the oldest collections of Icelandic traditions, compiled in the XIth and XIIth centuries, confirmed his testimony? The *Landnámabók* (Book of the Establishments) and the *Islandingabók* (Book of the Islands) do in fact say:—

" Before the island was occupied by the Norsemen, there were men there whom the Norsemen called *Papas.* They were Christians and it was thought they came from somewhere West of the Sea . . . they left behind them Irish books, bells and crosiers; that is why it must be assumed that they were Irish . . . and it is said in English books that at that time there were men who went away to these countries."

These chronicles add that the *Papas* left the country because they did not wish to remain in contact with the pagans, by which we must understand that Christian establishment founded by the Irish monks disappeared owing to the hostility of the Vikings when they had made themselves masters of the island.

The conclusion would seem to be that anchorites who came from green Erin to this unknown country, did so in order to bring Christianity to it. Others founded colonies across the islands of the Northern sea, which form, as it were, a highway between Scotland and Iceland. But to attribute this foundation to St. Brendan and to his companions is to move rather fast, for the only chronological indication which we have makes the settling of the Irish in Iceland about 795, when St. Brendan had been dead for more than two

---

[2] Identified with the most Northern of the Shetlands.

centuries. The hypothesis that St. Brendan came to these countries is drawn from a much later legend, which was probably composed when Iceland was already known. There is nothing in the biographical documents which can support this. The legend, furthermore, does not speak of their settling there: on the contrary, the good monks are only thinking of fleeing from these inhospitable regions, in which they seem to see the gates of Hell. As regards the question which we asked above; was St. Brendan connected with the original introduction of Christianity into Iceland? We must resolutely answer no, and conclude that the first evangelization of the great isle of ice owes nothing at least directly, to the founder of Clonfert; that this evangelization, about which there is nothing mythical, only dates from the years about 800, but unfortunately did not survive the arrival of the Norsemen, in the third quarter of the ninth century.

This whole development then proves historically, that beween the VIth and IXth centuries Irish monks, driven on by an irresistible desire for solitude, left their own country for the love of God, visited almost all the North Sea beyond Scotland and in numerous islands made foundations which lasted for some time. Unfortunately we lack the necessary details to give a definite picture of the activities of these first missionaries. One thing is always striking, the absolute confidence they all had in God when they gave themselves up to the waves. They accepted beforehand that it was His will, and at the same time they accepted the destination He had in store for them. It was this spirit which inspired Saint Columban when he set out on his travels which first took him to Gaul, then to Luxeuil, then to Bregenz, finally to Bobbio, making the sacred places come to flower beneath his feet, reviving the faith of our country (Gaul), spreading everywhere the true religion of Christ. It was this spirit which has given us one of the most extraordinary adventures lived for the service of God, that of St. Findan.

He was born in Leinster at the beginning of the IXth century. Brought up piously he also had dreamt of becoming a monk and leaving for unknown lands so as to spread there, through love of the Divine Creator, the doctrine of His Only Son, Jesus Christ. At that period, however, the Vikings had command of the sea, and blockaded the Irish in their island. These audacious pirates thought nothing of landing, pillaging the monasteries, burning the houses, and making away with the crops, the cattle and the women. In the course of one of their raids a band of Norsemen carried away Findan's sister. Fired by this insult, his blood was up. He vowed vengeance and that he would bring the young girl back to her parents. He intrepidly took to the sea, but soon he himself fell into the hands of the raiders

The drakkar which was taking him as prisoner towards the coast of Scandinavia, crossed between Scotland and the Orkneys: the crew now and then went ashore so as to keep their hand in. Findan resolved to profit by the situation: breaking his bonds he jumped into the sea, consigning himself to the mercy of God and vowing to go to Rome on pilgrimage if he succeeded in his attempt. God was well willing to help his servant; Findan landed safe and sound on the coast of Caithness, in the North of Scotland. The bishop of the neighbourhood received him and protected him. At the end of two years, he expressed a desire to fulfil his promise; he set out for Rome on foot, and, with the divine protection, he was able to complete his pilgrimage.

But Findan, like so many of his compatriots, had vowed not to return to his country. After Rome he stayed for some time at the Benedictine house at Farfa, but left in search of a " desert ". The retreat for which he was seeking he found in the middle of the Rhine, on the island of Rheinau, near Schaffhausen. This was in the year 852. He installed there a community of anchorites in the style of his country. He voluntarily condemned himself to the strictest seclusion and gave himself up to the most rigorous asceticism; he spent hours in prayer, in winter he refused to heat his cell, and frequently immersed himself in the icy waters of the Rhine. He died at Rheinau, on November 15th, 879, without having seen his native land again. A typical example of " travelling for the love of God ".

Saint Findan left to his companions at Rheinau a rule inspired by the one which St. Columban gave to Luxeuil; he also handed over to them a calendar and a missal which are preserved respectively in the university library in Zürich and in the library of Saint-Gall. In the calendar one finds references to numerous devotions to Irish saints, notably to St. Brigid of Kildare who became in this monastery the object of a cultus as fervent as it was unexpected, and also to St. Brendan the Navigator. St. Findan's was an original personality; he confided himself to the ocean, but then retired to the Continent to pursue the work of a St. Columban, a St. Gall, or a St. Killian.

We can then say, in conclusion, that alongside the admirable apostolic works which inspired monachism with a new life and which revived religious sentiment in continental Europe (Saints Columban, Gall, Fiacre, Fursy, Killian, etc.), there are other Irish monks, more obscure in their action, who equally worked to win the heavenly country " by the love of Christ ".

Instead of looking towards the Continent (with the exception, always, of St. Findan), they turned towards the ocean. Well ahead of the Scandinavians, they discovered the Faroe Islands and Iceland, maybe Greenland as well. They founded Christian institutions, but as we lack documents, we cannot tell the importance and degree of development of these. What we can conjecture, however, is that these institutions disappeared after the Norsemen invaded these parts. On the other hand, it seems equally certain that the Irish monks were more concerned with solitude, with prayer and meditation than with making converts, and that is certainly one of the reasons for the rapid disappearance of these establishments. This probably delayed for more than two centuries the conversion of Iceland. The frontiers of Christianity would have been pushed forward, and the civilizing work of the Irish would have been able to shed its radiance right to the extreme limits of the Western world, thanks to the intrepidity of those monks with hearts " bound with triple layers of bronze " who abandoned themselves to the grace of God and to the perils of the deep in order to reach the "heavenly country" by ways whose originality was certainly their most striking quality.

BIBLIOGRAPHY

Principal works consulted.
Sources:
1. *Vita Sancti Brendani Clonfertensis,* published in the *Analecta Bollandiana,* t. XLVIII, 1930, pp. 99-123.
2. *Vita Findani,* in the *Monumenta Germaniae Historica Scriptores,* t. XV, part 1.
3. Adamna: *Vita Columbae,* edition by J. T. Fowler, Oxford, 1920.
4. Dicuil: *De mensura orbis terrae,* edition Letronne, with *Recherches et critiques géographiques,* Paris, 1814.
5. G. Vigfusson and F. Y. Powell: *Origines Islandicae,* Oxford, 1905.
Studies:
6. Tachet de Barneval: *Histoire légendaire de l'Irlande,* Paris, 1856.
7. Dom Louis Gougaud: *les chrétientés celtiques,* Paris, 1911.
8. Dom Louis Gougaud: *Gaelic Pioneers of Christianity,* Dublin, 1923.
9. Dom Louis Gougaud : *Christianity in Celtic Lands,* London, 1932.
10. Dom Louis Gougaud : Article, *Celtiques (Liturgies)* in the *Dirtionnaire d'Archéologie chrétienne et de Liturgie,* t. II, part 2, col. 2969 to 3032.
11. Francis Carty: *Irish Saints in Ten Countries,* Dublin, 1942.
12. Daniel-Rops: *L'Eglise des Temps Barbares,* Paris, 1950.
Reviews:
13. *Proceedings of the Society of Antiquaries of Scotland,* Edinburgh, Vol. XXXI (1897) and XXXIII (1899).

Saint Columban and his Disciples

By *MARGUERITE DUBOIS*
Docteur ès lettres, lecturer at the Sorbonne

SAINT COLUMBAN, the most intrepid of the intrepid Irish
saints, who was, according to the words of Pius XI, " one of the
pioneers of Western civilization ", came of a noble family, about the
year 540, in the province of Lagenia (nowadays Leinster). Before
coming into the world, a portent had revealed the brilliance of his
destiny: flashing out from the glowing breast of his mother, a
symbolic sun revealed the splendour of his future radiance.

The monk Jonas, a biographer avid for details[1], has told us
nothing of his early years. We know nothing of his childhood. It is
however easy, in the light of the documents of the period, to recon-
stitute the atmosphere in which the little Columban lived.

A double education, that of nature and that of school, developed
in the child physical aptitudes and intellectual dispositions. Trained
in all bodily exercizes, a spirited rider, an archer and a jouster, he
also learn the secrets of animal life, seeking in the midst of the forest
the company of wild beasts. The work of the countryside attracted
him: he mixed with the peasants and the shepherds in order to glean
the lessons of an experience which was useful to him till the end
of his days. From the long periods of this practical apprenticeship the
child would return to his teacher, and gradually, as the years passed
by, he learnt to write, to read the psalter; he absorbed the rudiments
of grammar and Latin literature, of arithmetic and astronomy, of
philosophy and history. The Scriptures became familiar to him in
all their aspects, and his vocation as a poet made him find pleasure
in the study of prosody.

From adolescence onwards, Columban had thus attained a considerable degree of culture; it may be that his talents were already
rewarded with a certain celebrity, and Jonas tells us he was good-
looking.

So ardent a heart could not remain inert while his virile instincts
were awakening. Terrible temptations assailed the young man;
despairing that he would master them, he went for advice to a
recluse, who was celebrated both for her piety and for her wisdom,

---

[1] B. Krusch, *Vita Columbani Abbatis Diciplinorumique Ejus*, in *Monumenta Germaniae Historica, Scriptores Rerum Merovingicarum*, Hanover,
1905, Vol. IV.

and it was the voice of this woman which determined Columban to renounce for ever the vanities of the age. Scarcely had he heard the vigorous admonition of the anchoress than he determined to break with worldly life, to drag himself from the arms of his friends, to leave his well-loved parents for ever, and to enter a cloister so as to serve God.

Such a resolution could not be fulfilled without much pain. Maternal opposition was terrible and in order to cross the threshold of the house Columban had to push aside the prostrate body of his mother.

Surfeited with tears, those which he shed himself and which others shed over him, the neophyte left his own province for the island of Cleen, on Lough Erne, where stood the venerable abbey of Cluain Inis. After a wearisome journey, the young man at last knocked at the door. He was welcomed by Abbot Sinneill and took his place in the anonymous ranks of the servants of God. Dressed in the white habit, with his forehead mainly bare from the Irish tonsure, he received his shelter beneath a hut of clay, with a bed of hides, a stone pillow covered with straw, a bench and a wooden cross, and for light when darkness fell a peeled reed dipped in tallow. Columban received the riches of an absolute poverty.

Little by little the young monk incorporated himself in the unified life of the community; work, prayer, silence, mortifications. Still very young, after three years of probation and the complementary studies, the novice pronounced his vows: he solemnly promised to keep an absolute obedience, a chastity without weakness, and total poverty; up to his last breath he observed the law and had it obeyed.

At some time after that, attracted, no doubt, by the search for a more austere life, Columban left Cluain Inis to join the Abbey of Bangor, the famous "Valley of the Angels", situated in Ultonia (nowadays Ulster), by a deep bay. Three thousand religious were gathered together there; and it was quite a society in miniature which the young monk was going to join. In our day it is difficult to imagine this little world, isolated and compact, which, in order to be self-sufficient, contained bodies of all the trades, whereas the men of letters, the scribes, the illuminators and the scholars gave themselves to the work of the mind. In this industrious home there was an intense mystical life: long psalmodies, collective devotions, private prayers, superhuman penances. It was in the midst of so much spiritual glory that Columban was raised to the priesthood. It would seem, however, that no rest was given to this unsated soul. From day to day his vocation became more definite, and it was a missionary vocation. After long arguments with himself and with his superiors, Columban obtained from his Abbot permission to go.

He thus embarked, on a dangerous and unknown sea, a priest-sailor, accompanied by twelve disciples who were as fervent but also as inexperienced as he was. The sublime adventure had begun.

After a short call in Great Britain at the rocky coasts of Cornwall, the barque set sail for Armorica, and tradition says that the travellers landed near the village of Saint-Coulomb, in Ile-et-Vilaine, not far from the gulf of Saint-Malo.

The Apostolate in time took on such importance that the King of Austrasia, Sigebert, begged Columban to found a monastery in his territory. Inspired by heaven, the Abbot welcomed this request favourably and set out to look for a suitable site. Soon, in the March of the Vosges, in the frontier territory between Austrasia and Burgundy, amid impenetrable forests, the explorer recognized the remains of an old *castrum*, which had been deserted for a long time. It had formerly been called Anagrates; it became Annegray.

To try and describe the difficulties of every kind which met the Abbot and the twelve monks in trying to make a foundation would seem to be impossible: it was a struggle against virgin and rebellious nature, hasty sowings in badly cleared ground and sparse harvests before a menacing winter, then the cold, the wind, the snow, and before long, famine.

But miracle had begun to inhabit the Columban dwellings; on two occasions urged on by a heavenly vision, the neighbours brought them food; and the renown of these marvels brought to the Abbey a crowd of neophytes. Columban, assailed by visitors, importuned by the sick, could scarcely manage the essential hour for meditation. He then fled from the monastery, seeking for quiet right up to the heights of the mountains. There he would wander beneath the leaves, picking berries for his frugal meals; and the wild animals who lived in those places obeyed his laws; even a bear gave up his cave to him and became his faithful companion[2].

Soon, indeed, Annegray became too small to contain the crowd of novices who came there, and the master set out in search of a fresh foundation.

It was in the year 590 that Columban laid the foundations of the famous Abbey of Luxeuil, the home of heroism, holiness and light.

Gradually a monastery of vast proportions replaced the ruins of the pagan temple and the ruinous Roman fortifications. The church, which was consecrated by Bishop Aidus, held on high the fame of Saint Peter, the patron of the community; the guest-house welcomed numerous visitors; the workshops received famous specialists, and the

---

[2] This grotto, situated on a wooded hill, can still be seen in our days.

reputation of the school developed immediately, while the flow of the postulants increased. The number of monks increased at such a pace that they had to build, not far from Luxeuil, the daughter-house of Fontaines.

From then on those privileged spots became the centre of welcome for the most holy souls, at the same time as they became transformed into an extraordinary home of miracles. At the voice of Columban the rain ceased over the fields occupied by the harvesters; the most severe wounds were healed without leaving a mark; amputated limbs returned into position without pain; the barns became filled with grain; loaves and ale multiplied themselves; birds of prey brought back their victims; guilty men, with their hearts pierced by the insight of the holy Abbot, confessed their sins and amended their lives; even death itself sometimes obeyed the prayers of him who could hold it back and only struck with his consent.

It is not astonishing that such a flowering of wonders attracted to the Abbey the benediction of all. Careful to protect his religious from the temptations of pride, Columban had composed a very rigorous monastic-rule, which he applied without flinching and which his personal qualities made it possible for him to apply without revolt, for the leader, " austere in his tenderness, tender in his austerity", knew how to shade off by his sensibility the applications of too hard a law.

The peace, however, which reigned in the monastery was not long in being disturbed. Having regained for the faith the surrounding country folk, Columban judged that it was indispensable to convert the lords and the princes. Now the aristocracy were sunk in paganism and licence reigned at court. Urged on by his grandmother Brunehaut, a haughty and dominating woman, King Thierry had just repudiated his wife so as to give way entirely to the claims of his concubines. The scandal was enormous. Columban, who was greatly upset, knew what he must do; he would go and speak sharply to the monarch, even in his palace. At Boucheresse, at Epoisses, he took up a terrible position against the sovereign power, he cursed the king's bastards, refused the savoury dishes which the servants offered him, and triumphed for a time over vice and crime.

But this victory did not last long. The crafty Brunehaut knew how to arouse the animosity of the nobility and also that of the clergy against her adversary. She started by stressing the Irish quality which made Columban a foreigner, not to say an enemy, and which would have explained many of the differences of opinion and the clashes. She kept up old animosities, profited by misunderstandings and renewed old quarrels. The hierarchy in fact showed themselves very unfavourable in regard to this nationalist monk who had set up, in the March of the Vosges, a sort of monastic diocese with its own customs and laws. The higher clergy objected chiefly to the form of the Irish tonsure and to the custom of fixing the date of Easter according to the Anatolian cycle. Columban had supported his theories with excessive violence, and passions had not calmed down. Only a spark was needed to light the flame once again. The arguments of the queen and the great vassals ended by overcoming the king who allowed himself to be got round. Accompanied by a numerous suite Thierry claimed the right to enter the monastery which he wished to see open to all visitors, and as the Abbot forcibly opposed this plan which was contrary to the rule, the king deliberately violated the enclosure. A prophetic malediction immediately struck the fool-hardy prince, but in return the crime of lèse-majesté meant for the monk from Ireland prison and exile.

Columban at first succeeded in escaping from his guards; however, the protection of Heaven, which had been clearly manifested, placed no obstacle in the way of carrying out the sentence. Dragged away from his sons, the Abbot had to take the sorrowful road which would take him back to his own country. By special permission, the Irish and British monks accompanied him in his banishment; on the other hand the monks of Gaul were to remain confined at Luxeuil.

That walk to the sea was a long Calvary! At each step there was some marvel: deliverance of the possessed, surprising predictions, healing of the sick, the multiplication of food; but the greatest miracle took place at Nantes, when a storm arose in a period of calm weather, running the ship aground which was to take the Irishmen back to their own country. The sailors were much moved by this extraordinary adventure and landed the outlaws, when the vessel continued on its journey without hindrance.

Free once more and praising God, the monks took on once again with confidence their wandering life under the guidance of Him who had always guided them.

After having consulted Clothaire II, the King of Neustria, having blessed in passing the future St. Fare, and marked with an indelible seal Adon and Onen, Columban made his way to the Rhine, escorted by a large number of monks who were escaping each day from Luxeuil. Switzerland opened before them and Tuggen, washed by the waters of the Lake of Zürich, welcomed the wanderers who decided to settle on that enchanting site. From the start, however, the malice of the pagans placed difficulties in the way of evangelization. In vain did Columban break with one breath the bronze vase which contained the beer consecrated to Woton, in vain did Gall, the impetuous disciple, consign to the flames the temples and the idols, nothing could convert the infidels, and in order to escape death they had to leave.

Bregenz, the chief place in the Austrian Vorarlberg, was more welcoming, and the Irishman was soon able to establish a new monastery where peace and labour reigned. It was, alas, a peace troubled by many of the fears and sufferings which wounded the heart of the father separated from his sons. It was at this time that Columban wrote his most touching letters to distant friends, Hunald, Sethus and Fidolius.

Political difficulties were again darkening the horizon; fearing he would once more fall into the power of King Thierry, Columban judged it was dangerous to stay longer at Bregenz. In spite of the fatigue of age and the weariness of the days for him, the Abbot decided to respond, once more, to the Will of God, and he prepared for a fresh departure.

His idea was to reach Italy, travelling by the pass of the Septimer. This would mean a trying but not a dangerous climb, in spite of the height of the pass, which is up more than 2,300 metres. The crossing was however very arduous, and when the improvised Alpinists had reached Milan, their faces were haggard with fatigue. Agiluf, King of the Lombards, received them with favour. His kingdom had become a missionary country since the Arian heresy had spread, and the unhappy affair of the Three Chapters divided the Christians. From the time of his arrival, Columban took a vigorous part in the heart of this religious struggle and his interventions with the Papacy, daring as they were, nevertheless preserved all the vehemence and the sympathetic boldness proper to their author. All the clumsiness for which under these circumstances posterity reproaches the Irish monk finds its explanation or excuse in an essential truth: the faith which Saint Columban had in the Holy Spirit gave him in his own eyes a sort of infallibility. Passionately attached to the traditions of his own country, he defended them with intolerance because he recognized in them the Apostolic mark, something infinitely venerable. While he was submissive without reserve to the authority of the Holy See, he yet dared to reprimand the Pope, because he thought it is the duty of a son to enlighten his father and to safeguard his honour.

Thus, strong in conscience and almost certain of realizing on the soil of Italy the aim of his life, Columban decided to establish a monastic foundation on the site of Bobbio, a place wild and gracious at the same time. At the foot of Mount Penice, on the shores of the Trebbia, the work of clearing and building began without delay. With the multiple labour, the rhythm of the offices, and the incessant prayer there began once more the daily marvels: a bear submitted to the yoke to take the place of an ox it had eaten, an enormous wooden pole suddenly became light, whereas it had almost broken the backs of the monks who were carrying it. Every day there was a new dawn full of light, when grace enlightened the monks assembled round their leader, like vine-branches round the stock.

Nevertheless the sons had a presentiment that their father's life was nearing its end and that only the desire to see his work prospering still sustained him. Silently did they watch the encroachments of age in this man already so undermined by cares and privations. Nor were they surprised when the Abbot, begged by his disciple Eustasius, refused to return to Luxeuil, which was once more open to him since the death of Brunehaut and of Thierry. Everyone knew that he considered the risks of the journey too great and that he felt he had been vindicated by the hand of God, whose assistance he had sought. The punishment of the impious ones had been terrible, while the descendants of Thierry had been dispersed before the sovereignty of Clothaire who had reunited the whole empire beneath his sceptre.

The reigning prince who remembered the great merits and the wise counsels of the Irish monk, would liked to have seen him reinstating his monastery in the Vosges, but the old man, who judged that his end was near, wished to complete, in the solitude of his grottoes, the labours which were dear to his thought[3]. To his two master-works, the *Regula Monachorum* and the *Regula Coenobialis,* he had all through his life added homilies, sermons, letters and poems. From henceforth he would be completing his work, and the whole vast epic poem of his life appeared again before his eyes. He could, before he died, appreciate the result of his efforts as a whole and in their brilliance. How many monasteries had been built, shining with an incomparable lustre in the life of the century! How many wrongs had been righted and how much good had been accomplished! How many roads had been followed! What great sayings had been delivered to be meditated on by the humble and by Kings! How many hearts brought to submission and how many souls enlightened! How many destinies turned towards God, and what an astonishing influence in the multiple domains of politics, of faith and of civilization!

The day came when the holy Abbot felt the blood growing cold in his veins; he understood that the end of his troubles had come at last. He then called his minister and ordered that the monks of Bobbio should be assembled round him.

Jonas, who enveloped the childhood of Saint Columban in silence, covers with a similar silence the last hours of his earthly life. He only tells us that at dawn on November 23rd, 615, the monastery bell rang his knell. Columban the great had ceased to live.

:-:   :-:   :-:

When this noble figure had disappeared, the work of the master

---

[3] The grottoes of La Spanna and St. Michael.

experienced an extraordinary development across the world. His disciples, whether they remained in the monastery or were detached from the foundations, were to bring to Saint Columban's cause the help of their zeal and of their virtues.

Let us first of all mention Athala the Burgundian, Bertulf the Austrasian, and Bobolene, the son of Winioc the friend of Columban, all three faithful observers of the rule of Luxeuil, and on whom in turn depended the fate of Bobbio. This monastery, now deserted, became from the first century of its foundation, an intellectual centre of incomparable radiance; the learning and the holiness of the monks illuminated Northern Italy; the richness of its library astonished the world of the humanists, and for nearly a thousand years this privileged abbey experienced a marvellous extension.

However, if Bobbio had the special privilege of sheltering the ashes of the founder, it must not be forgotten that it was above all at Luxeuil that his thought developed and that the abbey in the Vosges was for three centuries the light of Gaul. Two of its greatest Abbots shared with their leader the reputation for learning and virtue which is the glory of the Columban monks. There was first of all Eustasius, a converted officer, formed beneath the rod of the Irish saint, attached to his superior by the most solid and the most spiritual of friendships, a noble spirit full of firmness and gentleness, an apostle with gifts for the work of the Gospel, a perfect master whose teaching bore fruit. There was also Walbert the Frank, whose admirable qualities as an organizer contributed to the success of the work and who in prudent fashion undertook to soften the founder's rule where it had grown too rigid.

It was in fact for wise men to modify, according to the needs of the moment and the welfare of souls, institutions which were too rigorous. Walbert thus renounced the customs of the Celtic liturgy of which Columban himself had abandoned certain features, also suppressing all divergences which were opposed to the customs of Gaul. Then he established the principle of stability, which held in check the frequently troublesome departures of wandering monks. In softening down articles which were too severe, such as penances which were too harsh, he received inspiration from the rule of St. Benedict who brought a precious correction to St. Columban's discipline. Indeed, in the course of time, most of the foundations of the Irish saint or his disciples gave birth to the most lively as well as the most famous Benedictine abbeys.

The tragic fate, which, in the VIIIth century, overtook the abbeys of Luxeuil, Annegray and Fontaines, when they were pulled down by the Saracens, scarcely darkened the sky of Columbanian monachism.

7 The Bock of Kells, details of an illuminated page.

8 The Book of Kells, an initial and interlinary illuminated.

A harvest of disciples made the name of the master live once more, and perpetuated his doctrine in all countries and ages.

On the soil of Alsace, Leonard founded a monastery which, about 724, restored by Máur, took on the name of *Maur Monasterium*, nowadays Marmoutier.

Desle the Irishman had not been able to follow Columban on the road of exile; he had succumbed to fatigue half-way along. God thus designed for him the scene of his labours. Collecting his remaining strength, the good monk went into the depths of the forest, dug into the earth with the end of his stick and having refreshed himself at a spring which appeared miraculously, settled near a little oratory dedicated to St. Martin. Every evening, when night fell, he would approach the chapel, the doors of which were always shut but opened to his voice. Having escaped from odious persecutions the cenobite came to have an extraordinary fame; disciples soon came to him, attracted by his preaching and by the brilliance of his knowledge. A monastery arose which quickly became famous and was enriched by the generosity of King Clothaire, and all the surrounding country profited to the full from the radiant atmosphere given out by this nursery of the saints. When the Abbey of Lure was able to do without the care of its founder, Desle retired to a hermitage where he gave up his soul on January 18th, 625. His virtues won him the title of blessed and his cultus still remains vigorous today.

In the course of Columban's travels across Gaul, another disciple was to detach himself from the group; this was Potentiu who established a monastery in the region of Constances (Manche).

On leaving Bregenz, when the monks were fleeing from the vengeance of the pagans, perhaps the most celebrated and the most impetuous of the Irish religious had to yield to an attack of fever and to renounce his journey. Columban, who misunderstood the attitude of his old companion, punished him severely by forbidding him to say Mass as long as he was alive. Such a punishment brought tears to the eyes of the sick man, but, in this unintentional injustice, the disciple, accustomed to bow to the will of his master, saw a decree of Providence. He accused himself of weakness, if not of indiscipline and received the decree humbly.

When he had seen his companions disappear en route for Lombardy, the unfortunate man who had been left behind placed his things on a boat and made his way to the house of a priest whose hospitality he knew to be generous. Willimar opened his house to him, gave him every attention, and soon brought him back to health.

However, anxious to find a solitude where he could serve God, Gall accompanied the deacon Hiltibod who knew the wild places of the neighbourhood. This cleric guided him as far as the banks of the

Steinach where the religious built his cell. In a short time the hermitage, furnished with a little oratory, became the embryo of a community where the most edifying holiness held sway.

One Sunday in November 615, the cenobite learnt by revelation of the death of St. Columban and received, shortly afterwards, the pastoral staff which his master on his death bed sent him as a sign of pardon. But Gall, now he was returned to the priestly life, did not renounce his solitude. He refused the office of Abbot of Luxeuil offered him by the monks of the Vosges, and died on October 16th, 646, surrounded by the veneration of all. His disciples continued the tradition of piety and silence which he had established, and in 720 the priest Othmar built, on the site of his cell, a monastery which was to be the home of medieval learning in Germany and in Helvetia.

Among the disciples of St. Columban who renounced following their Abbot into Italy was the monk Urcisin, the founder of Saint-Ursanne (Switzerland).

And there was Sigisbert, whose great age made long journeys out of the question, who went up the valley of the Rhine to found on Swiss soil, at Disentis (Canton of the Gusons), a monastery of brilliant renown.

Let us also mention the gentle gardener of Luxeuil, St. Valery, who became an apostle in the North of the country, and whose name is still connected with a magnificent work.

We have already spoken of St. Fare, a young virgin who received St. Columban's blessing, and who, governing the Abbey of Faremontiers, laid the foundations of something very fine. The fine example of this great Abbess drew to the Lord's service her brother Faron who, when he became Bishop of Meaux, generously endowed the Columban monastery of Sainte-Croix.

The prayers of Columban had in former times obtained the birth of a predestined child, vowed to God from his cradle. This was Saint Donat, a monk of Luxeuil, who, raised to the episcopal dignity, about the year 624, became Bishop of Besancon.

Three brothers, formerly noticed by Columban, were to answer with enthusiasm the call of him who had marked them out: Adon, the first, left the world to found the double monastery of Jouarre; Radon, the youngest, endowed generously the neighbouring house of Reuil. But what shall we say of Saint Onen, a high official of King Dagobert, who used all his influence to make the monastic spirit shine in Gaul? Under his protection Saint Aile became Abbot of Rebais, Saint Wandrille raised up Fontenelle, while Saint Philibert built Jumièges.

Among the less celebrated religious who were connected with Columban, tradition names the monk Chonon who was sent from the Abbey of Lerins to Luxeuil to study the Columbanian rule, and to bring the observance of it to his own monastery where doctrine had grown weak.

Later, when the direct influence of the founder had grown more remote, it was the disciples of the disciples who produced saints, thanks to that spiritual paternity; the fecundity of which seems to us nowadays so extraordinary. It would be in vain to try and enumerate here the many who continued a work which Providence had blessed, and each of these souls would merit a longer mention than could be given in this book. It is enough to have rapidly conjured up the fascinating Columbanian continuity that time has not been able to break.

Placed thus at the head of the holy group to whom France, Switzerland and Italy owed their religious expansion, Columban stands out as the striking figure of his century. In an age of brutality, his violence was fruitful; where the frenzy of the barbarians brought death, his thundering force brought life. He spoke, and the Kings bowed their heads, he cursed, and fear surrounded the guilty; he blessed and hearts linked themselves with his heart.

There was nothing in him which was not great. His vocation appears like a renewal of the lightning destinies which God of old reserved for His prophets. That is why, in spite of rocks and reefs, his work expanded with all its innovations: uninterrupted praise for the glory of God, auricular confession established long before the practice became obligatory, interior and exterior missions. But it would be impossible to understand Saint Columban without measuring him by supernatural values. It is values of this sort which give their meaning to the energy of the master, to the attachment of the disciples, and to the prodigious extension of the work. It is the same values which, fourteen centuries after his death, allowed the delegates of six grateful nations to group themselves round the name of Saint Columban[4].

In our days, indeed, his cultus lives again with fresh vigour. Each year it is celebrated at Luxeuil with a solemn festival, and it is the object of learned studies; Saint Columban is the patron of learned societies, and knows the glory of universal expansion. Italy has never ceased to honour his memory; Ireland, his own country, of which he remains the torch, Switzerland where he still is venerated, America

---

[4] From the 20th till the 23rd July, 1950, the united celebrations of the XIVth centenary of St. Columban, brought together at Luxeuil the official representatives, both lay and ecclesiastical, of Ireland, Switzerland, Austria, Italy, America and France.

and the countries of the East where his missionaries of today carry his standard on high, join with France in offering to the great evangelist the tribute of their gratitude and admiration.

The King of Love

The King of love my Shepherd is,
    Whose goodness faileth never;
I nothing lack if I am His
    And He is mine for ever.

Where streams of living water flow
    My ransom'd soul He leadeth,
And, where the verdant pastures grow,
    With food celestial feedeth.

Perverse and foolish oft I stray'd,
    But yet in love He sought me,
And on His Shoulder gently laid,
    And home, rejoicing, brought me.

In death's dark vale I fear no ill
    With Thee, dear Lord, beside me;
Thy rod and staff my comfort still,
    Thy Cross before to guide me.

Thou spread'st a Table in my sight;
    Thy Unction grace bestoweth;
And oh, what transport of delight
    From Thy pure Chalice floweth!

And so through all the length of days
    Thy goodness faileth never;
Good Shepherd, may I sing Thy praise
    Within Thy house for ever.   Amen.

Bibliographical Note: Consult M. M. Dubois, *St. Columban,* éd. Alsatia, Paris, 1950. To the bibliography contained in this work add the two important works following: *Mélanges Colombaniens,* Acts of the Congress of Studies held at Luxeuil on the occasion of the XIVth centenary of St. Columban, in July, 1950 (éd Alsatia, 1951) and *San Columbano e la sua opera in Italia,* Acts of the Congress of Studies held at Bobbio in September, 1951, (éd. of the Comité historique de Ialaisance, Bobbio, 1953).

Works, not yet published, are at this time in the course of production, whether at the French Abbey of Saint-Wandrille de Fontenelle (author, Dom Laporte), or at Los Angelès in California (author, Rev. E. J. MacCarthy, missionary of St. Columban).

Among the articles devoted to St. Columban or to his disciples, see in the Irish review *Studies,* the writings of Rev. A. Gwynn, S.J. (Vol. XXXIX, No. 155, Sept. 1950), and Rev. M. O'Carroll (Vol. XLII, No. 168, 1953); the study by Chanoine Cuénin in the *Revue d'Histoire Ecclésiastique Suisse* (1950, fasc. IV); that of Professor Vaccari in *Saggi di Umanismo Cristiano* (Sept., 1950), and the very numerous articles of Doctor A. Maestri, published by the Company of Oblates of St. Columban at San-Colombano-al-Lambro; and *St. Columban* by James Wilson.

The Irish Saints in France

By BERNARD GUILLEMAIN
Professor of the Faculty of Letters at Bordeaux

S CARCELY two generations had passed since Saint Patrick had evangelized Ireland when, on the soil of Gaul, there appeared the first islanders of whom we have the traces.

At the beginning of the VIth century, when the famous Bishop Rémi was occupying the See of Rheims, Gibrien installed himself on the banks of the Marne. Tradition ascribes to him six brothers and three sisters. One of these, Trésain, who in his case certainly existed, was placed in charge of the pigs, but he loved, so we are told, to draw near to the churches, to be present at Mass and to hear the offices. Struck by his piety, Rémi ordained him priest.

Fridolin came to Poitou, was Abbot of Saint-Hilaire, had the relics of the patron transferred into the restored basilica, then moved towards the East to visit Lorraine, Alsace, Burgundy and Switzerland before founding, on an island on the Rhine, between Basle and Constance, the double monastery of Säckingen.

When very old, Sézin, who in his youth would have known St. Patrick, received the divine order to cross the sea and went to Léon to spend the last years of a life of humility and patience. Boats, manned by his compatriots, would have gone alongside the Breton coast in order to take away his body, but, moved by the supplications of the inhabitants, left important relics behind, if not the whole remains of the old hermit.

These personalities arise in a night full of dreams. It is impossible to point out just where they start. How did a foreigner like Fridolin come to govern Saint-Hilaire of Poitiers? It is impossible for us to give the precise chronology. This same Fridolin, whose life was only written in the Xth century, is presented by his biographer as a contemporary of Clovis, whereas a modern scholar confuses him with a German who belonged to Saint Columban's entourage, younger by a century! What credit can we give to Gibrien's family or to the old age of Sézin, which the hagiographer prolongs to a hundred and twenty-seven years ? What particles of history are we to recognize in the legend ?

Detached from their country and from worldly goods so the better to win Heaven, ardent in penance, these saints of Ireland established their first shelters in wooden huts or the corner of a ruined

69

house. Their example at first surprised, then conquered the population; disciples perhaps joined them; the power of working miracles was granted to them; their remains have been venerated. A village in the neighbourhood of Châlons-sur-Marne is called Saint-Gibrien, and another, in Léon, Guic-Sezni, because the relics of St. Sézin were enclosed beneath the high altar. And, in 1600, Pope Clement VIII approved the office of Saint Trésain, composed at Rheims. For these humble men, these penitents, these men without history, popular piety composed marvellous adventures.

Many of the saints attributed to Ireland in the VIth and VIIth centuries—one hundred and fifteen in Germany, forty-five in France, forty-four in England, thirty-six in Belgium, twenty-five in Scotland, thirteen in Italy—who are thus signalled out by folklore, disconcert the historian but can prove their effectiveness. It was that they responded to the needs of the hour.

In Gaul, Christianity had won its cause to the heights of the social order, among the sovereigns and the great nobles; it was implanted in the cities, the walls of which protected the Bishop's house, the baptistery and the cathedral; churches had been established in the *vici*, straggling villages inhabited no doubt by free men. But a large part of the countryside was untouched, yet the country was essentially rural. The Bishops had opened some sanctuaries on their domains; proprietors had received permission to transform their oratories into churches. It was but a beginning; sullen and passive, dominated by their ancestral customs and superstitions, the peasant population could only be converted by the long presence of apostles, close to them in their way of living and feeling.

St. Caesarius of Arles, in the first decades of the VIth century, denounced the pagan festivities of January 1st; men used to disguise themselves as animals or as women; they exchanged new year's gifts and at night they loaded their tables with food, in the belief that abundance would reign with them throughout the year. They predicted the future while listening to the song of the birds. They avoided bathing from the time of the summer solstice. They feared Diana as the goddess of the witches and they did no work on the Thursday consecrated to Jupiter. The Councils of Orleans held in 533 and 541 forbade the eating of meat which had been offered to idols. They honoured trees, stones and springs.

If such survivals deserved to be pointed out in the South and the Centre, with even more reason was this the case in the North and the North-East. These were the regions where the bulk of the Frankish and the German people had installed themselves; they had not been converted. Even in the Ardennes were to be found the remains of the cultus of Wotan and Odin. The Bishoprics of the

Roman period, which had for a long time had no Bishops, were gradually reconstituted, but the Bishops were responsible for several Sees and had few and badly instructed clergy. To the North of the limestone hills of Artois, where the cemeteries give evidence of a relatively thick population though the towns were few and very small, there was a vast stretch of marsh, of heath and forest, the scattered and savage inhabitants of which seemed to discourage attempts at conversion to Christianity.

Who was to carry the Gospel to the Pagans or to make it practised by the baptized who were ignorant of its demands? It is only necessary to read Gregory of Tours, who lived from 538 to 594, to draw up a deceptive balance-sheet. The Kings, the sons and grandsons of Clovis, only thought of getting rid of each other. As regards zealous Bishops, devoted to their duties, there were too many great personages who only saw in the episcopate, opportunities for influence and wealth, and we even come across scandalous prelates, such as the brothers, Salonius d'Embrun and Sagittarius de Gap, degraded by the Council of Chalons-sur-Saône in 579 for homicide, adultery and lèse-majesté, or again the Syrian merchant, Eusebrius, who bought the Bishopric of Paris in 592. Monachism, that magnificent instrument, which was still a recent arrival, was already in danger of disorder; the wealth of the monasteries, which Princes, Queens and Bishops had founded and endowed, and the privileges they enjoyed, aroused envy. Finally, the density of these establishments would seem to be highly unequal; the North of Neustria and Austrasia were scarcely touched.

Then Saint Columban appeared; with him Irish monachism in Gaul was raised to the dignity of a historical force. He preserved the hermits' love of isolated places, even those where the country people gave themselves up to magical practices and revered the powers of nature; but to the disciples who flowed in he gave a rule of life. The monasteries of the island, which were adapted to a country without towns, where the clans remained the basis of the social structure, were not only refuges of peace and prayer; they were centres of worship and the homes of evangelization. Columban had not left Bangor solely to satisfy by the *peregrinatio* his ideal of renunciation and his roving nature; above all he desired to carry salvation to Gaul and to the neighbouring lands. He could dispense with the powerful; he accepted the gifts of the Kings but he attacked their morals; following the Celtic tradition, he refused the protection of the Bishops, admitting neither their control nor their jurisdiction, nor their way of calculating the date of Easter, nor their continental style of tonsure. He had only distant relations with the Holy See.

A profoundly original form of evangelization was thus making its

way in the Frankish kingdoms, quite different from that which was
being undertaken at the same time in Saxon England by the envoys
of Pope Gregory the Great, who were interested first of all in the
sovereigns.

To reach in its depths the population of the Northern half of
France, Ireland sent out her monks, independent and imperfect, who
avoided the courts and the towns, and took root in the midst of
nature; they understood the seduction of the waters, the forests, and
the rocks, but they did away with the mystery, and, carried away
by penance, they wore out their bodies so as to master their instincts
and to make their prayers more pure.

We know what was the radiance of that athlete of Christ, Columban, the founder of Annegray, of Luxeuil and Fontaine. In the same
wooded region, at the foot of the Vosges, one of his companions
remained when in 610 Brunehaut and her grandson Thierry drove
out the terrible Irishman: Desle, so his biographer tells us, wandered
in this wild country; he was tormented with thirst; he had knelt
down to pray when, before him, below the stick on which he was
leaning, a little stream of water gushed out. Desle built his hut there
—the first cell of the monastery of Lure. At the end of the XIXth
century, on the branches of the trees which cast their shade on the
spring, children's clothes could still be seen hanging, because the
water was reputed to cure childish illnesses. At the other extremity of
Gaul, Potentin had halted near Coutances.

Among the inhabitants of the Merovingian kingdoms, the spiritual
progeny of Columban was surprisingly numerous. Passing on to Briê
about 610, he halted near Meaux at the house of Agneric, the father
of Chagnoald who had joined him at Luxeuil and who was to become
Bishop of Laon; he blessed the two other children of his host, Fare
and Faron. When the young girl became of marriageable age and her
father spoke of marrying her, she became ill, then, having been cured
by Saint Eustasius, the successor of Saint Columban at Luxeuil,
she fled. Agneric agreed to recognize Fare's vocation, who, after
several years in retreat, founded between 617 and 627 on the lands
of her family a convent for women to which was linked a community
of men founded by monks from Luxeuil and destined to perform
priestly functions and to do the difficult work: Faremoutiers had a
widespread reputation; St. Berthille received her formation there
before ruling Chelles; about 646 the daughters of the King of East
Anglia and the daughter of the King of Kent retired there. Abandoned at the time of the Revolution, the convent was revived in
1931 by some Benedictines.

Faron, who occupied high offices at the court of King Clotaire II,
was elected Bishop of Meaux about 626. In the course of an episcopate

lasting close on half a century, he established in an area of his city a monastery of the Holy Cross, which he peopled with monks from Luxeuil—He became St. Faron.

Having visited the family of Agneric, Columban had stopped, a little before La Ferté-sous-Jouarre, at the house of one of the great ones of the kingdom of Austrasia, Authaire, and he had given his blessing to his sons, Adon and Dadon. These were important people. Adon left the court of Dagobert in order to found on the site of present day Jouarre, on the heights which dominate the Marne, a double monastery of men and women—These were governed by Theodechilde, who came no doubt from Faremoutiers and whose tomb can still be seen in the crypt of that convent to which the Benedictines returned in 1919. Dadon, better known under the name of Saint Oven, established an abbey at Rebais, before occupying the episcopal See of Rouen.

With Columban we can connect, whether directly or indirectly, a great number of the leaders and most of the foundations of that golden age of the Merovingian Church and of monachism, the sixth century. Saint Valery, who set up an establishment at the mouth of the Somme, had known the great apostle personally. Romaric, who founded Remiremont at the junction of the Moselle and the Moselotte, Berchaire, who in the Champagne country founded Hautvilliers and Montérinder, came from Luxeuil. It was from this astonishing reservoir of religious forces that Queen Bathilde asked for an Abbot for Corbie, that Besançon owed its Bishop Donat, founder of the monastery of Saint Paul, and Berry Theodulf, surnamed Baboleiu, and from which were borrowed the apostles of the North, collaborators of the great Saint Armand from Aquitaine: Achaire, Bishop of Noyon and Tournai, Omer, a Saxon whom Potentin had perhaps nourished in the faith and turned towards Luxeuil, who was promoted the first Bishop of Théronanne, Momeliu, who, before replacing Saint Eloi at Noyon, directed the Abbey at Sithiu to which Bertin, his companion, bequeathed his name, Ebertramm, the Abbot of Saint-Quentin, Théofroy, Bishop of Amiens, Aubert, of Cambrai-Arras. The Columbanian spirit animated the souls who desired personal perfection and missionary action: Count Wandrille prepared at Bobbio the foundation of Fontenelle and was ordained to the priesthood by Saint Omer; Philibert entered at Rebais, passed on to Luxeuil and to Bobbio before founding the monasteries of Jumièges, Saint-Benoit-de-Quincay, Noirmoutier and Montivilliers.

It has been possible to honour some forty foundations in the tradition of Luxeuil. And since one only lends to the rich, more than one hagiographer has attributed to his heroes an imaginary Irish origin!

Less striking than Columban, a little obscured in his radiance, other genuine islanders still followed in the VIIth century the roads of France, stick in hand, the head shaved in front from one ear to the other leaving only a half crown of hair above the forehead, the rest of the hair coarsely cut down at the shoulders, strange and majestic like the prophets, liking to build their huts near a spring or within the arms of a river.

Thus did Chaidoc and Fricor appear before the future Saint Riquier who was overcome for all time, thus the Scottish Bishop Flavinus before the future Berrichon Abbot of Longrey and Cyran. Saint Didier of Cahors, one of the great building and organizing Bishops, was an admiring friend of Arnanus. One, Thomeus, who was well known for his penances and his virtues governed round about 663 the diocese of Angoulême. One Sidonius, who has been made into Saint Saens, having followed Saint Oven, entrusted himself to Saint Philibert who gave him the office of cellarer at Noirmoutier, then the direction of the monastery which he was building in the valley of the Varenne about 684. Roding, following a pilgrimage to Rome, retired into the forest of Argonne; his reputation brought him competitors; this was the origin of the monastery at Beaulieu which he left not long before his death in order to take refuge in a neighbouring hut, where he could end his days in the solitude that he loved.

It is not easy to fix these dates. Was it in the VIIth century that there came from Ireland one of the most popular saints of our Brittany, Renan, whose name has entered into the composition of the names of people and places ? He would have lived on the heathlands of Menez-Hom, where a procession follows an immemorial route which is said to be his, and where his remains are venerated in the parish of Locronan. According to legend, when Queen Queban, who was jealous of the affection which King Grallo had for the hermit, had let her little daughter die while she was searching for her husband in the woods, and the people in their fury had stoned her, Renan brought both the Queen and the little Princess back to life.

However, in Brie, the Columbanian tradition which was so firmly implanted, attracted the Irish. Faron kept Killian in the monastery which he had established at Meaux, then advised him to join the teams which were evangelizing Artois; the Irishman settled at Aubigny near Arras. The same Faron granted some land, two leagues from his episcopal town, to Fiacre the solitary; it was the abbey of Breuil. Saint Fiacre was one of the best-known saints of ancient France. He was the patron of gardeners, he was invoked for various maladies, his name was used to baptize hired carriages for in the XVIIth century his image was to be seen on the mansion from which these came forth! It was said that he knew how to grow every sort of plant from the soil which he had cleared all round his hut, and that these nourished or healed travellers. Faron promised to give him the surface area which the hermit could surround in one day with a ditch. The Irishman had only to scratch the soil with his stick, the furrow sank on its own, here and there trees fell down and in the evening the perimeter was six times longer than any ordinary worker could have traced! The memory of these attractive stories lasted a long time. We hear of miracles attributed to St. Fiacre. Bossuet prayed to him for the restoration to health of Louis XIV, but as the Irishman had rigorously forbidden any woman to approach his dwelling, Queen Anne of Austria, when making a pilgrimage of thanksgiving for the cure of Louis XIV, was careful, even in the year 1641, not to enter the Abbey of Breuil.

As for Fursy, he does not seem to be a tributary of Columbanian posterity, and it is a pity that St. Bede the Venerable, who has described his visions of the other world, did not take the trouble to remind us of his earthly travels, which we can only guess at by means of a rather mediocre biography. From Ireland, Fursy first of all made his way to Suffolk. The entourage of the young King of Neustria, Clovis II, the son of Dagobert, was in relations with the Anglo-Saxons; the Mayor of the Palace, Erchinoald, had among his servants a young English girl, Bathilde, whom he had bought as a slave from some pirates; the reputation of Fursy no doubt reached his ears; the holy man was installed between 640 and 650 at Lagny, on the Marne. He kept to his frank way of speaking; he condemned the King and his "great men" who were immersed in vice, and we may think that he encouraged the vocation of Bathilde, whom her master Erchinoald had at first wished to marry, and who was finally given in marriage to Clovis II. He soon died and his remains were taken to Péronne in Picardy.

In his life-time Fursy was followed by several of his compatriots whose "Acts" are unfortunately far from reliable and whom he had directed towards the evangelization of the Oise country; folklore has preserved the memory of Saints Gobain, Algise, Corbican and Mauguille. When dead, he drew round his grave the constitution of an essentially Irish community, either a refuge or a halting place for the islanders who were seeking their salvation on the Continent: *Perrona Scottorum*. Foilan, his elder brother, started by ruling it but, having entered a lawsuit with Erchinoald, went to Fosses near Namur where he underwent martyrdom about 655. The younger, Ultan, returned to Péronne between 675 and 691. His successor, Celanus, who died in 706, is rather better known; a letter of his has been kept, to Aldhelm, Abbot of Malmesbury and Bishop of Sherborne, in which he asked for some manuscripts to distract the minds of his monks; some verses which he composed to be inscribed on the walls of the church proved that Patrick was honoured by this rather mournful group of voluntary exiles. Until 774 at least, Péronne remained in the hands of the Irish, perhaps till 880 when the house was destroyed by the Normans.

With the end of the VIIth century the rôle of the Scots in the Christianization of the Northern countries came to an end. Certainly, all superstitions had not disappeared. Pirmin, Bishop of Meaux, was still making a catalogue of them in the middle of the VIIIth century, as did the Council of Leptinnes in 744. The foundations of the Church had, however, been solidly laid; the institutions and the clergy provided a framework for the faithful who had transferred to the saints the privilege of conquering nature. The supernatural world was no longer a source of terror since it was known to be animated by God and friendly towards His elect. During this time of stabilization, Celtic monachism, which was both independent and farouche, was no longer what was required. Abbot Waldebert, the second successor of St. Columban at Luxeuil, had tempered and perfected the discipline which the founder had imposed on his disciples, by borrowing largely from the rule of St. Benedict which demanded less from the monk, and organized better his life in community. It was this mitigated rule which from the second third of the VIIth century had been adopted by the monasteries of the Merovingian kingdoms. In the following century the adoption of the Benedictine rule became general; was it not marvellously well-balanced? Was it not at Fleury, on the banks of the Loire, that the relics of the patriarch were housed, after the destruction of Monte Cassino by the Lombards?

The relations of the episcopate and the regular clergy became arranged in a different way from that defined by the Irish. If the monastery was protected from the abuse of episcopal power after the Columbanian example, it did control a religious district as was the custom in the island, and it no longer disposed of "claustral Bishops", subordinate to the Abbot, and only destined to fulfil those functions that only Bishops could perform. Mazerolles, Stavelot, Saint-Denis, Saint Martin of Tours had in the VIIth century counted among their numbers prelates who conferred Holy Orders on religious, and consecrated churches and their altars.

Saint Boniface, who reorganized the Frankish Church, no longer tolerated wandering Bishops, who passed from diocese to diocese and ordained priests. They were indispensable in a missionary country and period, but they no longer had their place in a stabilized clerical society, where the canonical principle ruled of one Bishop for each diocese. Some of them even awakened suspicions, shewing signs of a doubtful orthodoxy and even demanding money for rendering their services. Did not a certain Clement reject ecclesiastical celibacy in order to recommend the customs of Judaism ? Did not a certain Samson preach that Baptism was of no value for salvation ? In 744, the capitulary which was published after the Council of Soissons required that all itinerant prelates should be examined and authorized by the Ordinary. In 813, with a special eye for " the Irish who say they are Bishops ", the forty-third canon of the Council of Chalons-sur-Saône declared that ordinations performed by them were null and void.

This is the proof that the islanders continued to wander about the Continent. But they were for the future rather on the margin of ecclesiastical life. Most of it escapes us. Alongside the bad there certainly were the virtuous ones, noticed here and there, and who had honourable careers, such as Abel, the Abbot of Lobbes, who in 744 was raised to the Metropolitan See of Rheims, or Hélie who died as Bishop of Angoulême in 860. Rome attracted these indefatigable pilgrims. Killian, Roding and Saens had visited the threshold of the Apostles. In the Xth century Malcallan, after praying at the tomb of St. Fursy, kept two houses in the Ardennes and in Thierarchy where travellers were received. Tradition tells of these companions: Cadroc, Fingen, Lazare. How many were there who went on the same journey ? In the XIIth century, on the return journey, two Archbishops of Armagh died on French territory: one, Malachy, died in 1148 in the arms of St. Bernard, who spoke magnificently of him; the other, Concord, ended his days in the Benedictine priory of Lemenc, on the hill which dominates Chambéry, in 1175, and a confraternity was established under his patronage in the XVIIth century; in 1854 Archbishop Dixon, his distant successor, took back to his fatherland a relic of this saint who had been forgotten for so long by his compatriots!

However, Ireland, having for the space of a century, given life to the mystical invasion of the pioneers who gave new vigour to the monachism of Gaul and saved the Christian seed among the rural peoples of the North, rendered a second service to the West. Its monasteries preserved intellectual culture. When Charlemagne undertook to set to rights the studies which were indispensable for the spiritual efficiency of the clergy, he did not think merely of the Italians and the Anglo-Saxons, but also of the Irish. About 782 arrived Clement, who was to draw up a Latin grammar, and another personage who is either one of the Dungals, who were experts in astronomy and philosophy, or else the poet, Joseph the Scot. This was the start of a new invasion, that of letters, which established its colonies at Cambrai, at Rheims, at Soissons and Laon . . . " The only really thoughtful head " of the IXth century, said one who knew well, was John Scotus Eriugena, who knew Greek and who, between 845 and 870, in the time of Charles the Bald, translated the Pseudo-Dionysius and composed in the Platonic form of dialogue a treatise *De Divisione Naturae* (Of the Division of Nature) which, until the century of St. Thomas Aquinas, provided the vocabulary of philosophical language.

After the adventures of those who cleared the ground, of the missionaries and the heroes of asceticism, this was something quite different, and the second gift from Ireland to the civilization of the Christian West.

Saint Columban, Saint Gall and the Formation of Switzerland

By GONZAGUE DE REYNOLD

CENTURIES of incubation are needed for a country to form, and centuries of preparation for it to reach political independence. This accession is the sign of its maturity. Beforehand, it could be seen disengaging itself little by little from the vast mass in which it existed in a potential state. To this slow, very slow release, I would readily ascribe the Augustinian theory of seminal causes and reasons. Their manifestations *ad extra*, which at first are not numerous, become multiplied in a given geographical space, then they become rejoined, and co-ordinate with each other. A system of relations is established. Then a new people, a new nation appears.

The mission of St. Columban and of his disciples is for Switzerland one of these seminal reasons. That is what I wish to show. For that reason, I will limit my subject just to this mission without launching out on a study of the Columbanian influence on the present-day territory of the Confederation.

I

This mission has its history and its legend. They are to be found entwined with each other in the *Vita sancti Galli*.

The *Vita sancti Galli* is the work of a monk who belonged to the Abbey of which the Irishman had been the founder and who lived at the end of the VIIIth century. The Zürich historian, Meyer von Kuonan, published it in 1869 in the *Mittheilungen zur Vaterländischen Geschichte*, as volume XII; B. Krusch has included it in the *Monumenta Germaniae*. For the reader's pleasure and my own, I am going to translate this text, shortening it, and at the same time tidying it up a little.

:-:   :-:   :-:

After the check to his mission in Gaul, Columban went to Austria to King Théodebert who also possessed the Helvetic countries, and who allowed him to come and also to work for the glory of the Lord.

Columban had the idea of leaving some of his disciples with the Alamans and to go on himself as far as Italy. Having thus crossed

79

the Rhine, they moved upwards towards Limmat and stopped at a
castle called Turégum, which later became the town of Zürich. This
castle looked out on a lake, the shore of which they followed till
they reached a town called Tuccinia or Tucconia, nowadays Tuggen.

Tucconia was inhabited by pagans. Columban and Gall set out
to evangelize them, these pagans assembled around them. They
listened to these foreigners without understanding them; when
Columban or Gall pointed towards Heaven, they raised their eyes
towards the clouds and only saw the clouds or the birds flying.

The place pleased the monks from Ireland, but the monks from
Ireland did not please the inhabitants. This is how it was:—

The pagans of Tucconia worshipped three great wooden idols.
Now, Gall, in his zeal, took a torch, knocked over the idols, and set
fire to them. There was an upheaval with cries of anger. The monks
had to fly in haste. Columban, who was of a certain age, ran slower
than his disciples. The pagans caught him, turned him over and
beat him with rods, after which they left him. Columban got up
and cursed them.

:-:   :-:   :-:

Columban and his companions pursued their journey through
forests and across mountains. They reached the lake of Bodan, at a
village surrounded by walls: Arbona, today Arbon. A holy priest
lived there, Willimar. Willimar saw them and ran to meet them,
saying: " Blessed are those who come in the name of the Lord! The
Lord my God has visited me ". Having embraced them, he took
them into his house.

After seven days of rest and edifying conversations, Columban,
talking to Willimar, asked him:—

" Do you know of a place in this country where I can retire with
my disciples and work for the conversion of the barbarians ?"

" I know of a solitude where the earth is good," was Willimar's
reply.

Columban said: " Will you lead us there?" whereupon Willimar
took his stick and led his companions to the other end of the lake
of Bodan.

:-:   :-:   :-:

Willimar led Columban and the eleven others into the region of
Pergentia, now Bregenz. This fertile land had already received the
seed of the Gospel but there had been wars, the priests had left
without returning, and the people had lost no time in falling into
idolatry. Idols had been placed in the Christian church. Learning
from the experience of Tucconia, the Irish did not overturn them

A

B

9 (A) Initials of the Book of Kells. — 9 (B) Initials of a manuscript of the 8th century ;
illuminated in the N.E. of Gall. (Paris Latin 13 159.)

B

LIBER
GENE
RATI
ONIS

ihūxpi filii
dauid filii abra
ham; Abraham
genuit isaac;
isaac aut genuit
iacob; Iacob aut
genuit iudam et frs
eius; Iudas aut genuit

A

at once. They started by establishing themselves, by making themselves useful, by preaching gently, then more strongly. At last the day came when Gall could break the images; he even poured out a vase containing five hundred measures of beer destined for Wotan, the traveller God, who is also Odin.

Half the pagans murmured, the other half was converted. The church was purified and dedicated to St. Aurelius, whose relics Columban carried with him and which were sealed in the altar-stone.

:-:   :-:   :-:

However, the demons who infested the country tried in vain to reach Gall who was protected by the sign of prayer and who was ceaselessly vigilant. That is why, as they were unyielding, they resolved to be revenged. They inspired Cunzo, the Duke of Alemannia, with bad thoughts against the monks. Now, Cunzo was a pagan. He ordered Columban, Gall and the Irish to leave the country under pain of death. Columban had regrets for the country and the good soil and he said: "We had found a golden shell, but it was full of serpents. However, do not be discouraged; God will send His angel to guide us into Italy; there we shall meet with a generous King who will give us a home."

When on the point of leaving, Gall was suddenly attacked by a fever. He placed himself at Columban's knees and declared to him that being tormented by a violent illness, he could not follow him. Columban understood that God wished to retain His chosen one, Gall, within the confines of the Alamans, for the salvation of the barbarians; he said: "I know, my brother, that it is painful to share my labours. Remain here, but remember this: as long as I am living in a mortal body, you will be forbidden to celebrate Mass." He commended his disciple to Willimar and left.

:-:   :-:   :-:

The holy priest Willimar had entrusted two of his clerics, Maginold and Theodore, with looking after Gall and caring for him assiduously; this they did. When God's chosen one had been cured of his fever, he sent for the deacon Hiltibold, another of Willimar's companions, and said to him:

"My son, do you know of a remote spot in this region? I desire with a great desire to end my life in solitude."

Hiltibold answered him: "I know a remote spot; but it is wild, surrounded by high mountains and inhabited by fierce animals, wolves, wild boars and bears."

Gall stood up. " God, Who delivered Daniel from the lion's den, will defend me against the wild beasts; He will guide us as He guided Tobit. Come, my son, let us make our way into the forest."

:-:   :-:   :-:

Gall and Hiltibold set out fasting, for Gall had sworn to take no food till God had shown him the chosen spot. They penetrated deeply into the forest. About midday, they stopped on the edge of a torrent, where there were more stones than water, the Steinbach. Having enjoyed some rest, Gall rose up to continue the journey, but his foot became caught in the brambles, he stumbled and fell. He then recognized the will of God and cried out: " Let us go no further, my son, let us remain here! This is the chosen place, here I shall live till my death!" He took a branch of hazel wood, broke it, made a cross, planted the cross in the earth, and hung on it the relics which he had on his chest, the relics of St. Mary, St. Maurice and St. Desiré.

Hiltibold then said to him: " My father, we must now have some food." Gall said: " Let us start by lighting a fire ", and they collected some dead wood when a bear came out of the forest. Hiltibold was seized with fear, but Gall turned towards the bear. " Bear," he commanded with authority, " I order you in the name of Jesus Christ; go and fetch us some wood for our fire." The bear obeyed; he turned back, and then returned with some wood which he threw on the fire. Gall then blessed him and let him go.

Gall said to Hiltibold: " My son, the fire is ready; we only lack something to eat. Take your nets and go down to the river."

When Hiltibold drew near to the river, he saw between the trees two naked women who were getting ready to bathe. He saw them and temptation stirred his flesh. But the two women, having turned round, mocked at him, because he was deformed; they threw pebbles at him. Hiltibold made the sign of the cross and said this prayer: " My Lord Jesus, Son of God, have mercy on me a sinner and drive these demons far from here." And the vision faded.

Gall drove all the other demons from the forest. For several days they could be heard lamenting and crying out in the distance among the mountains, but each day the voices were less near and soon there was silence. In the same way Gall drove out the serpents which were numerous and which disappeared from the countryside. Helped by Hiltibold he built a hermitage and an oratory. He received a visit from Willimar.

:-:   :-:   :-:

Gall had twelve disciples with him. Now, when they were all asleep after singing Matins, the chosen of God awoke with a start and waking up the deacon who was alongside him, he said to him: "Magnoald, prepare everything that is necessary for celebrating Mass, for I have just had a vision and I know that my blessed father Columban is dead."

When the Mass had been celebrated, Gall said again to the deacon: "Hasten, and leave for Italy. You will go to the monastery at Bobbio and you will find out exactly about the death which has delivered my blessed father Columban and led him to eternal glory."

Magnoald left and went to Bobbio. And he found out exactly. Then he came back, edified, with a letter in which were related all the details concerning Columban's death. He also brought back to Gall Columban's stick.

:-:   :-:   :-:

The little monastery which Duke Cunzo had built for the chosen of God grew yet larger, for the chosen of God did not cease receiving new disciples. Gall was now aged; he was ninety years old.

The priest Willimar was still alive. He had begged Gall to come to see him, for he also, Willimar, was aged and felt that the end was approaching. The chosen of God yielded to Willimar's request and left for Arbon. But scarcely had he arrived when he was attacked by a malignant fever; he died and his soul flew away to the abode of the saints.

The Bishop of Constance, Jean, being warned that illness had struck down the chosen of God, hastened on the way. He met people who were weeping; he understood that the chosen of God was dead, and he also wept.

He had preparations made for the funeral. As he was distributing Gall's clothes to the poor, it chanced that he gave the sandals to a paralytic. Scarcely had the latter put on the sandals when he stood up and began to walk.

They had dug the grave, but no human force could lift the coffin. Then Bishop Jean said: "In truth I recognize that this place, reserved for our father in which he might rest, is not the proper place."

He then ordered two wild horses to be harnessed to the wagon which was carrying the coffin, with their bits removed, and the horses led the wagon and the coffin to the cell of the Chosen of God.

II

The *Vita sancti Galli* needs a commentary. I will apply it to what concerns my subject, the part played by St. Columban and St. Gall in the formation of Switzerland.

:-:　　　　　　　:-:　　　　　　　:-:

What is Switzerland in herself ?

On the relief map of Europe she appears to be like a little free space which nature has inserted between Germany, France, Italy and the Danubian countries, like a pebble between four blocks of granite, as if it intended to reserve it for a people independent of these four entities. To the North lies the great moat of the Rhine; to the East and South the bastions of the Alps with their moats and their encircling roads, to the West the blue wall of the Jura; that is the framework.

What had history already made of the free space at the date when Columban and his disciples made their way there ?

To answer is to sum up the long history of Switzerland before the Swiss.

The Helvetii have written the introduction. This Celtic *natio* formed part of the vast and loose Gallic confederation; its situation on the border, behind the Jura, allowed it to act with almost complete independence. They had not taken the risk of penetrating into the Alps, which was the domain of the Rhaetii, but they had installed themselves on the plateau, from Geneva to Winterthour. In the VIIth century, their memory continued in the name of Helvetia and in the adjective Helvetic, as stated at the beginning of the *Vita sancti Galli*.

It was the Romans who wrote the most important chapter of the history of Switzerland before the Swiss. Having collected together under their domination the two parts that made up the free space, the plateau and the Alps, they made the free space the centre, the cross-roads of their empire of the West. They did this by linking it with Italy, Gaul, Rhenish Germany and the Danubian countries, by means of the rivers, the Alpine passes and above all by their celebrated roads. They surrounded Switzerland like a belt having its buckle at Milan. It was divided into two areas, to the West, that of Helvetia, to the East, that of Rhaetia. From the first there issued a road which ran along the feet of the Jura, from the second a road which ran along the Rhine. They joined at Augst, in Latin *Augusta Rauracorum,* a colony of veterans, quite near Basle. From there they united in the great road which went along the Rhine towards Mainz on to the delta of the river and its mouth in the *Mare Germanicum.*

At the time of our Irishmen, the Roman roads were always used, at least the chief ones; but they were badly kept up, and " the roads for walking " were preferred. Columban and his companions entered the free space in 610-611 by the gate of Basle and the Rhine. From the Rhine they went up by the Limmat till they reached the Lake of Zürich. They had arrived near Tuggen, in what is nowadays the canton of Schwyz. In Latin, Tuggen has the name of *Tucconia* or *Tuccunia,* or to be more exact *marca Tuccunia,* for it was then on the line of demarcation between the Austrasian Franks and the Alamans. When the missionaries arrived, Tuggen was a village of boatmen who lived by the transport of merchandise on the lake.

From Zürich, Turegum, the Roman road followed the right bank of the lake till it reached that of Wallenstadt, which interrupted it : Wallenstadt and Wallensee signify the town and the lake of the Welchi, that is to say the Reto-romans. At the other end of the lake, the Roman road took up again, at Maienfeld (in Latin *Magia*), joining up with the great road coming from the lake of Como, crossing the Julia, coming down to Coire, *Curia Raetorum,* and ending at Bregenz, *Briganticum,* at the extreme Eastern end of Lake Bodan or the Lake of Constance. There it joined up with the Rhenish road going towards *Augusta Rauracorum.* Columban took the great Rhaetian road when he left Bregenz to go into Italy. For his part, Gall settled not far from Arbon, that station on the Roman road. But let us return.

The chapter which followed that which Rome had written in indelible ink, was that of the barbarians, that of the Germans. Alamans and Burgundians, these mortal enemies, shared the free space. The first, in the name of the empire of which they were federates, settled in the Western part on the strength of a legal settlement. The second advanced from the Rhine to the Alps, by incursions followed by clearing of the ground.

Alamans and Burgundians were successively overcome by other Germans, the Franks. When the Irish arrived, the Merovingians had remade the unity of the free space, apart from Raetia, which, under Clovis, was held by the Ostrogoths of his brother Theodoric.

III

I have just named Clovis and Theodoric . . . The King of the Franks had managed to overcome the Alamans who were to him a danger just as they had been a peril for the Romans. Theodoric had managed to save a few remnants which he had established in Lower Raetia. It was there that St. Columban and St. Gall were to find him.

:-:   :-:   :-:

Now that the Franks had overcome the Alamans, their work was to civilize them. But to civilize meant also to Christianize them.

The enterprise was far from easy, for whether overcome or not, the most barbarous of all the continental Germans obstinately continued to show themselves hostile to Christianity and unamenable to civilization. They shut themselves up in that exclusiveness of tribes and regions which had made for their weakness when faced with the Franks.

Merovingian policy thus proceeded wisely and slowly. At the end of the VIth or the beginning of the VIIth century the See of Strasburg was founded. At the same time they set out to repair the damage for which the Alamans were responsible in the free space, where they had overthrown the ecclesiastical organization. In Alsace, the See of Strasburg had already been founded. That of *Augusta Rauracorum* was transferred to Basle; a new See was founded at Constance. But let us look at the map. Between the See of Constance and that of Strasburg, the See of Basle is on the peak of an angle of which the Rhine forms the two sides. On the right there stretches out the great portion of Alamannia, that of Suabia. The episcopal Sees thus seem to us first as fortresses, then as the bases for evangelization.

No doubt the Frankish kings had lands in Alamannia. They entrusted the administration of these to Christians. From the VIIth century onwards the Dukes of Alamannia had been baptized. Several of their subjects had followed their example, indeed had even received Holy Orders like the priest Willimar, the friend of St. Gall. But many of the Christians had, for lack of priests, relapsed into paganism; for example, those whom St. Columban and St. Gall found at Bregenz in the act of drinking beer in honour of Wotan and in company with idolaters.

The mission of St Columban and his disciples had begun about 610-611; Columban had abandoned it in order to go down to Italy about 613-614. This mission would thus have been very short and it would have been brought to an end if Gall had not remained in the country. In spite of that the evangelization of Alamannia was not undertaken methodically till the following century. It was the work of St. Pirmin, a Visigoth from Spain or Aquitaine. The Merovingians had already been replaced by the Pippinides. The formidable Mayor of the Palace had Alamannia dependent on him. He had not wished to know anything of St. Boniface. On the other hand he entrusted Pirmin with the work of organizing and bringing to life this Church of Alamannia which, up to now, had only existed in name. To achieve this, Pirmin, the itinerant Bishop, became the founder of monasteries. The first which he established in 724 was the famous Abbey of Reichenau on the Lake of Constance. It was to be one of the great homes of the Carolingian renaissance, and of the renaissance under Otto—the latter being the revival and the completion of the former.

The two other great centres were to be Fulda and Saint-Gall.

IV

The Abbey of Saint-Gall has an origin, a pre-history and a history. This I shall now sum up.

:-:   :-:   :-:

The origin is the hermitage which the favourite disciple of Columban built for himself in the forest of Arbon, near the Steinbach, the " stony torrent ".

The pre-history of the monastery which thenceforward was to bear the name of its founder, is as obscure as the forest. We know enough, however, to affirm that the life was hard. There were still pagans living in the forest of Arbon. They attacked, invaded, pillaged and burnt the little wooden monastery so that about 712 it disappeared.

Yet its history was only just beginning.

:-:   :-:   :-:

About 720, the governor of the district, with the consent of Nebi, a successor of Cunzo, and the assent of Charles Martel, charged Otmar, a priest of Alaman origin, but who had been formed in the Bishopric of Coir, to rebuild the monastery and to reintroduce conventual life. Otmar introduced the Benedictine rule, but he provoked the hostility of the Bishop of Constance, who found him too independent. He was deposed and imprisoned on a tiny island on the Rhine, near Stein. He died there on November 16th, 759, and was not long in being canonized.

I shall divide the history of Saint-Gall into three periods.

The first I shall call Carolingian: Charlemagne, who was interested in the Abbey, maintained it as a dependancy of Constance. In 854, Louis the German gave it back its immunity. According to a register of 895, the Abbey had 101 monks, of whom 42 were priests. They were all free men and almost all Alamanni. At that date, the territories of the Abbey stretched as far as the other side of the Rhine, to Suabia and Bavaria.

Thanks to its prosperity which permitted it to do things on a wide scale, and thanks to the high reputation of its school, Saint-Gall entered on what is known as its golden age. This was especially the case under Abbot Salomon, who died in 920. But let us stop in order to enter that Abbey which is already so large, so as to see what a centre of civilization was like at that time.

This civilization was formed round the spiritual principle which is the religious life. In three ways: By the arts, the culture of ancient traditions and the development of the vulgar tongue. The monastery itself represented architecture. The sculpture is represented by Tutilo's diptych, in which there stands out in ivory a beardless Christ with undulating hair, enthroned between the four Evangelists and their symbols, and the mythological figures of the earth and the ocean, the sun and the moon. The gold and silver work is to be found in Abbot Immo's antipendium. The paintings are seen in the celebrated Irish manuscripts which belong to the origins of our modern painting. A catalogue of the ninth century cites thirty-two *Libri* and *cottice scripti;* the finest is the famous *Codex Fifty-one,* whose decorative virtuosity contrasts with the barbaric lack of skill betrayed by the representation of the figures.

If we pass on to the ancient letters the whole Carolingian renaissance is in the translations and the commentaries which Notker III, known as Labeo, gives us of Boethius, Terence, Virgil and Aristotle. But we must not forget that Notker himself is one of the greatest poets of his time, the poet of the sequences. Let us now pass on to the vulgar tongue. The interlinear translations of the psalms, the texts of the *Pater* and the *Credo,* the glossary of Kero the monk, the famous vocabulary of Saint-Gall; here indeed are the beginnings of the German tongue. There is more to be said; the Abbey played an important part in the development of German epic poetry. It possesses one of the two manuscripts of the song of the Niebelungs. Finally, the doyen Eckhard put into Latin verses, inspired by Virgil, the story of Walter and of Hildegonde, that fine branch of the great oak the *Germanisches Epos.*

The second period is feudal. It issues from a crisis, the incursions of the Hungarians who pillaged and burnt the Abbey in 937; there was economic distress and a slackening off in religion. Reconstruction was slow and constantly held up, but the XIIIth century marks a fresh height.

An abbatial state was formed which was dragged into all the conflicts and all the struggles of the time.

There also grew up, however, the town of Saint-Gall, which was made rich by the cloth trade and industry. Like all the others, it laboured to extend its frontiers. It constituted itself into a little territory where it was sovereign, which made a state within the state. It surrounded itself with walls which separated it from its Prince-Abbot. It governed itself on the lines of the Swiss towns, in a way that was popular and patrician at the same time. It allied itself with the

Confederates. It embraced the Reformation. The division was then completed. From then on we have the Town and Republic of Saint-Gall, protected by the Protestant cantons, by this title a member of the Helvetic body. It disputed in the federal diets just like its former sovereign, whose representatives were jostled by its delegates.

During the third and last period, the princely period, the situation of the Abbot in his monastery was like that of the Pope in the Vatican. He resided before the walls of a town which used to be his, of a town begotten by his monastery, but which had turned him out as if he were a foreigner. To make up for this, this foreigner reigned over a territory with perhaps 90,000 inhabitants. In the XVIIIth century the abbatial territory was a model of organization, especially from the military point of view. The Prince-Abbot was a faithful ally of the Swiss, which did not prevent him from being an equally faithful member of the Holy Roman Empire. In 1648, the Prince-Abbot refused to recognize the divorce between the Confederates and the Empire.

In 1798 the armies of the Directoire invaded Switzerland, where they spread terror. The Abbot and his monks fled to Austria. They came back in 1799 and left again in 1802. In 1803, the formation of the canton of Saint-Gall put an end to the monastery. In 1833 a Bishop was installed in the Abbey, after many difficulties.

V

Saint-Gall was not the only lasting foundation which the Irish mission left behind it: there was Disentis.

:-:   :-:   :-:

A disciple of Saint Columban but who had a Frankish name, Sigisbert, took leave of his master that he also might bury himself in solitude. But he went much further away than Gall: across High Raetia, or Raetia de Coir, he reached the mountain mass of Saint-Gothard.

The mountain-mass of Saint-Gothard is a cross-work of valleys: to the North, that of the Reuss, to the South, that of the Tessin, to the East, that of the Rhine, to the West that of the Rhone. Between the two first there is a pass through which at that date no road passed, scarcely even a path leading to the pastures: between the two others, right below the pass, the little vale of Urseren, in Retoroman Ursera, opened like a passage raised up by a few steps between two great corridors.

The little vale of Ursera, which could be called etymologically the valley of the bear, thus put in communication, across the Alps of the

Saint-Gothard, the two great valleys of the Rhone and the Rhine,
which made it possible to pass from Lake Leman to Lake Bodan in
the shadow of the mountains. It is the "central furrow" of the
geographers. The Romans had fully understood its importance and
had opened it up.

:-:   :-:   :-:

Sigisbert settled in the Ursera, and set to work to evangelize its
few inhabitants. He then went down to the Upper Rhine valley to
found in a deserted place the Abbey of Disentis, in Latin, Desertina.
This was in 614. He was aided financially by his disciple Placidus,
who died a martyr about 640. This Placidus was rich, for he belonged
to the Victorides, Franks whom the Kings had established in Raetia
as *praesides*. Several Bishops of Coire have come from that line.

The site of the monastery was not left to chance. It was at the
branching off of two Alpine roads, that of the Oberalp which kept
it in communication with the Ursera, and by this with the Rhone,
and that of the Lucmanier (the great Luke) which linked it with
the valley of the Tessin and by this means with Upper Italy—without
forgetting that Disentis was itself on the Rhine road.

The emperors, I refer to those of the Holy Roman Empire, attached
great importance to the Alpine passes: were not these so many
doors opening between Germany and Italy? Also the two first, Otto
and his son, Otto II, made important donations to Disentis. Henry III,
in 1048, granted it imperial immunity. Henry V confirmed this in
1112, and Frederick Barbarossa in 1154.

The fact was that the emperors were engaged on a transalpine
policy; to keep a firm hold on these gates of communication between
Italy and Germany, to facilitate movement between the North and
the South; they built bridges, set up hospices, they repaired old
roads and opened up new ones.

The chief of these new ones was the Saint-Gothard road. It had
the advantage over all the others that only one pass had to be crossed
to go down from the Germanies into Italy and to go up from Italy
into the Germanies. To do this it was necessary to have the boldness
to throw a bridge across the abyss of the Reuss: it was the Devil's
Bridge, the first suspension bridge in Europe. The Abbots of Disentis,
who held in fief the valley of the Ursera, set to work on this along
with the people of Uri and the Léventine. They built a hospice at
the Saint-Gothard as they had already done at Lucmanier.

The opening of the Saint-Gothard road was not only of economic
and religious importance, but also of political. It brought into the
general life the two *Marktgenossenschaften* of Uri and Schwytz. It
thus gave birth to the confederation of the three *Waldstaetten*, that
first form, that attractive form of the Swiss confederation.

VI

When the Western empire collapsed, and the free space was given up without defence to the Burgundians and the Alamans, there was in Switzerland, as in the whole of Europe, an empire to replace it—the Church. The ecclesiastical organization maintained the unity of faith and the unity of organization in this parcelled out country; the monks established two large schools: to the West, that of Saint-Maurice d'Agaune, to the East, that of Saint-Gall. In the first, Gallo-Romans and Burgundians, in the second, Alamans and Raeto-Romans, received a common education in a common faith.

Saint-Maurice and Saint-Gall were not slow to co-ordinate: did not Gall have with him relics of the chief of the Theban legion ?

It was in the valley of Ursera that the cults of the two saints met. Legend tells that the " valley of the bear " was evangelized by a companion of St. Maurice before being so by a companion of St. Gall.

But the valley of Ursera is the centre of Switzerland.

The Irish in Belgium

By *HENRI DAVIGNON*

of the Academie Royale de Belgique

IN 1639, a professor of the University of Louvain, Nicholas Vernulaeus, put together the names of thirty-nine Saints who came from Ireland to Belgium, to which had been added those of three Saints; but when one examines from near this imposing list, one finds, says Père de Moreau, "that a certain number of these Saints did not live in the seventh century, but later; and that the Irish origin of several others is very problematical; finally, that with a few exceptions, their actual careers, and in particular their participation in the evangelization of Belgium, are only known by later sources which are scarcely worthy of belief."

It is certain, however, that in the victory of Christianity over pagan forces a part must be granted to isolated evangelists, neither attached to an Abbey nor to a diocese of the ancient Belgium, and in this group some Irishmen were distinguished, Scotti, as they used to be called. An author has described them as " supernumeraries of the Scottish emigration ". To the small value of the Belgian sources on this subject we must add absence of all mention of their names in the ancient Irish martyrologies.

Legend on the contrary, today attributes to these saints from beyond the sea the foundation of churches, and the persistence of pilgrimages to their sanctuaries, to those picturesque places, and there are even traces of processions of which folklore attains living tradition. The Catholic hierarchy respects these devotions, it takes part in them down to their most original displays, such as those "military marches" of the Sembre and the Meuse. The exotic origin of these fabulous people contributes to them prodigious merits and acts, and their qualification as princes, as sons of kings, is in favour of a popularity for which the excessive zeal of the clerics, often writing several centuries after the moment of their presumed appearance, adds a hagiographical interpretation.

Of these Merovingian *vitae* learned men have explained the birth and the arbitrary fortunes. This leaves them nonetheless admitted by popular devotion. If it is difficult to make out to what real persons they refer, one can admit certain signs and the ascetic quality of the virtues which are held in honour, the religious influence of the unknown Irish missionary and the spiritual filiation of the monastic doctors such as St. Columban, of whom St. Amand, the great Belgian evangelizer, claims descent.

There is no talk of a Church of Belgium, just as one talks of a Church of France, or a Church of England.

The regions which today bear the name of Belgium, have had by their geographical configuration, by their position of being between political and military currents from which Europe emerged, an aspect of their own. The missionaries who uprooted paganism, and sowed the Christian faith, had to take account of this. In the framework of the first diocesan organization, in the social and religious action of the monasteries, in the repercussions on the ecclesiastical life of the events of the great movements of ideas, the Christian soul which reveals itself and comes to flower, verifies itself by the aspect of contemporary Catholicism. The importance of these first centuries has remained of great importance, it explains the behaviour of souls and one will find in it the trace of Irish asceticism.

Father de Moreau has written a Life of St. Amand, whose name is held in great veneration in the region of the Escaut. " By the duration and the fertility in his ministry," he says, " St. Amand surpasses the first Bishops who worked with him for the conversion of a part of Belgium . . . he alone fully merits the title of Apostle of Belgium." He was born in Aquitaine, received his first literary formation in the monastery of the Island of Yeu, and lived as a recluse after having received the tonsure at Tours. It was there also that he asked of God, in conformity with Irish practices, that he should no longer see his country and might spend all his life in *peregrinatione*. He was a Bishop without a fixed See, the country that Amand set out to snatch from paganism was precisely that of the West, situated to a large extent in Belgium of today (that which is watered by the Lys and Escaut). The author of *The Life of St. Columban,* a cleric of Noyon, revealed that this Saint lived for three years helping St. Amand in his apostolate " on the ship of the Scarpe and the small boat of the Escaut."

The influence of St. Columban preponderated in almost all the monasteries which were founded in Belgium at that period. Following the Irish and their imitators the monks burned to become voluntary exiles. Several were hermits, such as St. Rombaut. He had been son of a King of Ireland and had been consecrated Archbishop of Dublin. Before announcing this dignity at the hands of the Sovereign Pontiff, he left for a distant region where an angel made him see the crown of a martyr and he thus arrived at Malines where he founded an Abbey.

The abundance of monasteries across Belgium reveals, especially for the group at Nivelles, Andenne and Fosses, a close dependence

on Irish monachism. Saint Itte, towards the end of her life, herself
called to Fosses three brothers of Irish origin: Fursy, Feuillien (or
Foilan) and Ultan. Feuillien, who is still popular today, was killed
by brigands.

The Irish conception of a monastery entailed a greater independence
of religious in regard to diocesan Bishops. It was under its influence,
direct or indirect, that several Belgian Abbeys obtained in the seventh
century and at the beginning of the eighth "charters of liberty".
It was also in these Abbeys that there prevailed the idea of Abbot-
Bishops with a greater liberty of movement since it was a question
of carrying their missionary action outside their Abbeys.

If the Abbeys of women are less numerous than the Abbeys of
men, they were not founded by kings or by princes, but by rich
relations or holy women. Gertrude of Nivelles, who was concerned
with deepening the contemplative life, inaugurated the exercise of
Lectio divina with the help of doctors who had come from across the
sea. These Irishmen also formed a community of men alongside that
of the virgins. The double monasteries often lived under one direction.

The ascetic life spread outside the monasteries. Merovingian
hagiography has retained the memory of men and women who lived
as hermits. Their renown for virtue and heroism often made them
have a tragic ending. Thus were born several legends of which the
source is to be found in the realities which issued from the imitation
of Irish asceticism.

I will only quote one which is to be found today in a country
which is partly de-Christianised, but which has a persistent belief
in it. It is that of St. Rolende of Gerpinnes. In her *vita* published by
Jean Gielemans (1427-1487) and composed it seems in the twelfth
and thirteenth century, she is presented to us as the daughter of one
Didier, who held rule over the peoples of Gaul. She was asked for
in marriage by Oger, the son of the King of Ireland. She refused and
fled. Wishing to go to Cologne she stopped in order to rest, with
the three people of her suite, in the " Villa de Gerpinnes ". She soon
left, but being more and more worn out, she had to stop at a farm-
house at " Villiers " where she died. Following a miracle, the clergy
and the chief people of Gerpinnes moved her body into their church.
It is still there and the casket which contains it is solemnly processed
on each Whit Monday, on the territory of several parishes, escorted
by soldiers, wearing the military uniforms of several different periods.
Their leaders are elected and take this ephemeral command very
seriously.

The strange thing is that a neighbouring parish claims to have the
remains of Oger, the Irish prince, who would have been suitor for the
hand of Rolende; the two feasts coincide, and the two processions meet

at certain points with their escorts. " Saint " Oger also has a casket. At one moment that of Rolende begins to run across a wood carried by vigorous youths who are dragged along, in memory of the flight of the virgin, before the pursuit of the fine prince. The bearers of Oger's casket rival the speed of those of Rolende's reliquaries. One day, says a contemporary chronicler, the two silver chests knocked against each other and one heard on each side the bones groaning. Such is the miracle in popular imagination. It is true that through the ages it is poetry which has carried it on. The Ireland of the Saints is no stranger to that of Walloon folklore.

Irish Missionary Work in Scotland and England

By REV. JOHN RYAN, S.J.,

Professor of Early Irish History, University College, Dublin

T HE death of St. Patrick is likely to have taken place about the year 460. A hundred years later the Church in Ireland could be said to be in an exceptionally flourishing state. The ascetical spirit, which St. Patrick had favoured, and which found its natural expression in monasticism, was everywhere in evidence, to such an extent, indeed, that monks, rather than clerics, and abbots rather than bishops, were the most prominent figures in the native ecclesiastical organization. At first sight this might seem to be an obstacle to missionary activity, for the purpose of the monk, as his name proclaimed, was to sanctify himself in silence and solitude, not to sanctify others. The centre of his life and thoughts would be a cell and a narrow monastic enclosure. In Ireland, however, there were influences that made isolation well-nigh impossible. To begin with, the monasteries were normally parish churches and the monks the parish clergy of the people. Thus the monks were kept perforce in daily contact with the faithful. Again, the monks had a rigidly severe concept of the religious life. The need for ruthless self-conquest was accepted as a first principle. Now exile was regarded as a cruel mortification and therefore a very meritorious form of self-renunciation. Hence its special appeal to the more generous-minded. They would leave their beloved country, never to return, and journey abroad as pilgrims for Christ's sake. And once abroad they would act as their brethren had always been accustomed to act at home, by providing the people among whom they lived with spiritual ministrations. Irish ascetical tradition demanded that those who had entered on the way of perfection should devote themselves zealously to the work of procuring the salvation of souls.

The first object of their attention, outside their own country, was the western coast of what is now Scotland. In the sixth century that part of the island of Britain was occupied by four nations. To the north were the pagan Picts, a pre-historic people; to the west, in Argyle and the islands, were the Irish, recent colonists from Antrim; to the east were the pagan Angles, yet more recent colonists from Scandinavia; while south of the Firth of Clyde dwelt the Britons, ethnologically one with the indigenous population who had formed

96

A

B

11 (A) An initial of the Second Bible of Charles le Chauve
(Paris, Latin, 2).
11 (B) Gospel Book No. 51 of the Library of St. Gall.

the Roman province of Britain. It was an obvious duty of Irish church-men to minister spiritually to their own countrymen who had settled beyond the sea. An extension of their interest to the pagan Picts and Angles was also to be expected. This, in fact, happened: Irish monks and clergy, using the Irish colony as a base, scattered as missionaries into Pictland and, in due course, into the Angle kingdom of Northumbria in what is now England.

In the great work of the conversion of Scotland the most important name by far is that of St. Columba of Iona. He came to that island " pro Christo peregrinari volens ", in 563. Other Irish missionaries may have preceded him in the area. Iona lay on the border of Irish and Pictish territory and may have been claimed by both peoples, for St. Columba seems to have obtained a grant of the site from both Irish and Pictish kings. It proved to be a very convenient missionary centre. Adamnan tells of a visit paid by St. Columba to the Pictish ruler, Brude, at his capital, afterwards called Craig Phatric, " St. Patrick's Rock ", near Inverness. With Columba were two other Irish saints, Comgall of Bangor—himself a Pict, and therefore, presumably, a speaker of the Pictish language—and Cainnech of Aghaboe, whose church, Cill Chainnig, gave its name to the present county of Kilkenny. The prominence of St. Columba in the conversion of Scotland may be judged from the number of churches dedicated to him in later times. Reeves, in his edition of the *Vita Columbae* by Adamnan, enumerates fifty-six, to which Forbes in his " Kalendars of Scottish Saints ", adds two. St. Brigid, the chief woman saint of Ireland, has the next largest number, while St. Cainnech, who is known to have co-operated with St. Columba in missionary work, comes third. Sailor saints, who gave their assistance, were St. Brendan of Clonfert, hero of the *Navigatio Brendani*, and St. Cormac ua Liatháin. Finbarr gave his name to the island of Barra; St. Flannan to the islands—Eileanan Flannain—of the Hebrides west of Lewis. Very remarkable is the multitude of dedications to Irish saints, Ciaran of Saigher, Fínán Lobar of Swords, Fínán of Lindisfarne, Comgan, Donnan, Fergus, Faelan (Fillan), Ethernasc, Berach, Beán, Blathmac, Blaan, Maelruba, Senan, and so on. By the seventh and eighth centuries Irish monks had churches everywhere on the mainland and the greater islands while Irish hermits occupied the barren rocks and inaccessible places along the Scottish coast, in the Hebrides, the Orkneys, the Faroës. They even visited Iceland. A study of the calendar of the saints of Scotland makes it abundantly clear that Ireland is the Mother-Church of that country. About four-fifths of the Saints are Irish or derive from Ireland. The remaining fifth represents chiefly the church in Strath-clyde which goes back to St. Ninian and the Roman Province of Britain and produced one eminent evangelist, St. Kentigern of

Glasgow, in the sixth century. Connection between the Irish Church and the Church in Scotland remained inexpressibly close until the end of the eleventh century, when the King of Scotland, Malcolm III, who had married the exiled English princess, St. Margaret, succumbed to her influence and allowed her to anglicize, in many respects, the Church of his fathers.

To the Irish and the Britons, then, Scotland owed its conversion to Christianity. In that glorious work the former outdistanced by far the latter. Among the Irish leaders the most distinguished was easily St. Columba of Iona. Hence it is difficult to gainsay his right to the title traditionally accorded to him, " Apostle of Scotland ".

Before St. Columba died, probably on June 9th, 597, the conversion of the Anglo-Saxons had been undertaken by Pope St. Gregory the Great. His instruments in this perilous task were St. Augustine, the monk, and a group of brethren from the monastery of St. Andrew on the Aventine. Progress was slow. When Justus, the fourth Archbishop of Canterbury, was consecrated in 624 the mission, after 27 years of zealous effort, had not extended beyond Kent, and even in that small kingdom, had given no certain signs of permanency. Ethelburga, sister of the King of Kent, married Edwin, King of Northumbria, in 625. He was a heathen, but his queen received permission to practise the Christian religion without hindrance. She had taken with her as chaplain Paulinus, one of the Kentish missionaries who had been consecrated bishop. When Edwin was converted to the Christian faith, Paulinus was given an episcopal See at York. At this time Northumbria extended from the Humber to the Forth and was the most powerful of the English states. Its preeminence was resented. In October, 633, Edwin was defeated and killed by Penda, the pagan king of Mercia, and Cadwallon, a Christian prince from Wales, who had a number of old scores to settle with the Northumbrians. Edwin's kingdom was now devastated. The two near relatives, who became his successors, apostatized, but within a short time they were slain. Paulinus, with the Queen, took to flight. They went on board ship and journeyed by sea to Canterbury. Save for a simple deacon, too insignificant to excite hostility, the Church in Northumbria had been annihilated.

Edwin's nephew, Oswald, who had been educated at Iona, now took the field against Cadwallon. Towards the end of A.D. 634 the rival armies met at a spot called Heavenfield and victory rested with the Angle king. Cadwallon was slain in the encounter. Oswald on the throne proved to be an admirable ruler. He is described as a man of pure and noble character, able as an administrator and exemplary in his habits. The first object of his rule was to bring the whole nation over which he had begun to reign under the influence of the Christian Faith. He called on Segéne, abbot of Iona, to help him in this work. A bishop was despatched from the island monastery but he soon returned in disgust, protesting that the Angles were so barbarous in their ways that it was a waste of time trying to convert them. One of the monks questioned the validity of this judgment. Did not St. Paul, he asked, emphasize the need of giving milk to babes and not expecting too much of people reared in paganism ? All eyes turned on the speaker, a monk named Aidan, who thus seemed designated by God's Providence to become the leader of the mission. He was consecrated bishop and sent to Northumbria in the summer of 635. Results were to show that no better man could have been chosen for the post. He fixed his episcopal See, not at York, but on the little island of Lindisfarne, a site that reminded him of his beloved Iona. Lindisfarne soon became one of the great Christian sanctuaries of the country, " locus cunctis in Britannia venerabilior ", to cite the words of Alcuin. From the " Holy Island " of Aidan and his successors Christian life was to radiate over all the Northumbrian realm; later too over the great midland district of England and ultimately to the territory of the East Saxons.

Bede can hardly find words in which to express his admiration of Aidan's beautiful character. His gentleness, piety, ascetic moderation, absolute other-worldliness, made a deep impression on his flock. His person was a powerful recommendation of his teaching. When at home in Lindisfarne his daily life was that of a mortified monk. A liberal supply of helpers, imbued with his own apostolic spirit, was sent to him from Iona. Their work was blessed with success. From among the new converts, Aidan selected twelve boys to be trained for the service of the altar. One of these was to become in time the celebrated St. Chad, patron of Lichfield. Aidan spoke English imperfectly but the king knew Irish well, thanks to his long stay in Iona, and often acted as interpreter. His gifts to the missionary were given at once as alms to the poor.

All went well until August 5th, 642, when Oswald, who had been at war with Penda, pagan king of Mercia, was surprised by that fierce warrior and slain. His death was generally regarded as a martyrdom, so that he appears as St. Oswald in the calendar of the English Saints.

Northumbria, as a single kingdom, did not survive Oswald's death. Oswy, his brother, succeeded to the northern portion, Bernicia; Oswin to the southern portion, known as Deira. As was to be expected, these events reacted unfavourably on the mission; yet Northumbria continued to be, during the seventh century, the backbone of the Church in England. Oswin became the intimate friend of St. Aidan, until his murder in a civil war with Oswy in 651. A few days later

St. Aidan took ill as he was visiting a church on the outskirts of Bamborough. He was laid on the bare ground, supported by the wooden buttress of the oratory, and there, in a poverty and detachment worthy of his Divine Master, he breathed his last.

When news of his death reached Iona a monk, Fínán, was consecrated as his successor. In virtue, in zeal and in ability as an organiser, he was worthy of St. Aidan, so that the Church in Northumbria grew and prospered. Oswy, now king of the whole realm, had married a Kentish princess, whose private chaplain insisted on celebrating the Easter festival according to the Continental system of reckoning. From this the Irish system differed. To the ordinary trials of Fínán's episcopate there was added therefore for a while the bitter cup of the Paschal Controversy. But the work of propagating and consolidating the Christian Faith was not seriously impeded.

At Fínán's death in 661 there were six monasteries in Bernicia and six in Deira, including those at Gilling, Tynemouth and Lastingham; the two at Tadcaster and Hartlepool and the famous double monastery at Whitby, ruled over by St. Hilda. Further north was a foundation at Old Melrose, where Eata, one of the twelve boys trained by Aidan, was already abbot. With religious centres so many and so powerful it is clear that by 661 the Christian Church had become firmly established in the whole Northumbrian kingdom.

St. Fínán was succeeded by St. Colman, also a monk of Iona. During his episcopate the dispute about the Easter date came to a head. As is well known, this thorny subject had caused immense trouble through the centuries since the earliest days of the Church. Owing to the fact that Alexandria enjoyed a high reputation for mathematical and astronomical studies, the mode of reckoning evolved in the Church of that city was widely accepted. But Rome had a system of its own, said to go back to apostolic times and cherished accordingly. When the two systems gave a different Easter date, there was great annoyance and disturbance. On occasion, Rome accepted the Alexandrine date or the two Sees agreed on a compromise. Strange to relate, a third system of reckoning seems to have prevailed in the Roman Province of Britain. It is thought to have come to Britain through Gaul from the Orient, for nothing corresponding with it is found anywhere in the West. From Britain it was carried to Ireland by St. Patrick and his missionaries. It remained the common mode of reckoning in Ireland in the sixth century, despite the efforts of various Irish churchmen to replace it by the Victorian Cycle or the Dionysian Cycle from the Continent. In 457, Victorius of Aquitaine had sought to combine the traditional Roman system of reckoning with the Alexandrine system which was then recognized as mathematically the more accurate. In 525, Dionysius Exiguus, an Eastern monk living in Rome, drew up a new cycle, which frankly accepted the main principles of the Alexandrine system. It is not certain that this cycle was adopted immediately but it is clear that by the end of the sixth century it was the official cycle in the Eternal City. A generation later, about 632, it was accepted in the southern half of Ireland. The northern half of the island, with Iona and through that monastery the missionaries in Northumbria, retained the ancient Romano-British system.

King Oswy decided to settle the question in his kingdom once and for all. He summoned, therefore, a number of churchmen to meet him at Whitby in 664. Bede calls this gathering a "synod", but it was in fact a royal conference, for the three bishops present were no more than counsellors. Two of these were in favour of the Iona cycle, so that if the meeting were a synod that cycle would have prevailed. But King Oswy, who presided, gave the decision in favour of the Alexandrine Cycle, for the excellent reason that it was the cycle then used by the successor of St. Peter in Rome. St. Colman regarded the verdict as an affront to the learning of Iona. He retired thither with a number of disciples, Irish and English, to discuss, Bede relates, his future line of action with his ecclesiastical brethren. In fact he never returned. The English monks who accompanied him found a new home in Ireland, where their monastery, Mag eo na Sacsan, "Mayo of the Englishmen", gave its name to the present county of Mayo.

Irish influence in Northumbria did not cease with the retirement of St. Colman. Many of the Irish missionaries accepted the Whitby decision and remained at their posts. The new Bishop of Lindisfarne was Tuda, who had studied in Ireland, and may have been an Irishman by race. At St. Colman's request, Eata of Melrose, one of the twelve boys formed by St. Aidan, was transferred to Lindisfarne as abbot. When Theodore of Tarsus, sent by the Pope as Archbishop to Canterbury in 669, divided Northumbria into two dioceses in 678, he placed Bosa, a monk of Whitby—where the tradition was completely Irish—as bishop in Deira. At the same time he nominated Eata Bishop of Lindisfarne and Hexham.

Another Irish monk, St. Fursa, had been active as a missionary among the East Angles. He built, to use Bede's words, "a noble monastery" at Chnoberesburgh (later Burgh Castle) in Suffolk. With him there were his two brothers, Faelán and Ultan, and two Irish priests, Gobbán and Dicuil. In this area the Church made slow but sure progress. Sigebert, the King, left his throne for a monastery in 635. When the state was invaded by the heathen Mercians, he refused to leave his cell and put himself once more at the head of his troops. Dragged to the battlefield by force, he refused to use arms and was slain. Somewhere between the years 640 and 644, Fursa journeyed to Gaul, where he built a monastery at Lagny in Neustria. There he died about 650.

The first mission to the English midlands was despatched by St. Fínán of Lindisfarne in 653. It consisted of four priests. One of these, named Dimma (a pet form of Diarmuid) was consecrated bishop in 656. " In a short time," as Bede relates, " he won not a few to the Lord." At his death he was succeeded by another Irishman, named Cellach, who was consecrated also by St. Fínán. Political changes led to the return of this bishop to Ireland. His two successors, English by race, were consecrated and sent to the Mercians by the Irish Fathers in Northumbria.

Even to the West Saxons, in their kingdom of Wessex, Irish influence penetrated. A Frank named Agilbert, who had gone to Ireland " legendarum gratia scripturarum " was named Bishop of Dorchester in 650. Owing to continued difficulty in learning the Saxon tongue, he left England, retired to Gaul and there became Bishop of Paris.

An Irishman who, about 670, won renown in Wessex, was Maeldub, " in erudition a philosopher " who had been attracted by the beauty of a peninsular hill named Ingleborne and had obtained leave to build a hermit's cell beneath its slopes. He was a learned man and round him a community grew that was to develop into a great monastery in honour of our Lord and Saviour and of his chief apostles, Peter and Paul. The place, Maeldub's Burgh, softened by Saxon lips into Malmesbury, retained its founder's name. He and the Irish missionaries who went before him, zealous workers who spent themselves in the conversion of the heathen English, are commemorated by Newman in his " Idea of a University " (p. 16) in a passage of exceptional beauty. An Anglican scholar, Dr. Lightfoot, exaggerates when he states that " Augustine was the Apostle of Kent; Aidan was the Apostle of England ". Yet there is a sense in which it would be true to say that St. Aidan holds the first place in the evangelization of the English people. Irish activity was responsible for the conversion of the Angles in the north; it had much to do with the conversion of the midlands (Mercia) and of the east (East Anglia); it was felt even towards the south, in Wessex. The way was thus made easy for the able archbishop, Theodore of Canterbury, who gave England a hierarchical system that transcended state and racial boundaries and welded the country firmly into the comity of nations that was Christian Europe.

Irish Spiritunlity in Antiquity
By REV. FULBERT CAYRÉ, A.A.

I. THE ANCIENT IRISH MONACHISM[1]

THE antiquity of which we are talking here covers the period which goes from the fifth to the twelfth century, that is to say from the conversion of Ireland to St. Malachy, contemporary and friend of St. Bernard. With him comes to an end the transition of the ancient forms of monachism to a preponderant Benedictine influence, when the hierarchy also imposed their will in the Church of the country. The ancient spirituality must be closely connected with monachism, in Ireland, more no doubt than in any other country of that period. It is first of all to the number of monks and to their action that the title of isle of the Saints is manifestly due, which was given it in antiquity and which was so well merited.

The Christianization of the island as a whole took place in the fifth century, and it is remarkable that from the beginning of the sixth the country was covered with large monasteries, but already in the time of St. Patrick the foundations had been laid[2]. He was the true promoter; at the same time that he set out to establish in Ireland the hierarchical organisation, he had himself had direct contact with monachism at Lerins, where he stayed for some time in his youth, after his captivity in Ireland. No doubt also in his native land, in the south of great Britain, Christianity had been implanted and had had relations with the East: the Britons were not afraid of travelling. At the time of St. Jerome they volunteered to go on pilgrimages to the Holy Places. Now a pilgrimage of this kind, usually entailed, whether on the way, or on the way back, an excursion to the solitaries of Egypt, whose angelic life amazed the West. Besides, Palestine was herself rich in monasteries. St. Simeon Stylites (that miracle of the Universe, as he was called by Cyril of Scythopolis),

---

[1] General Works: Gougaud, Dom Louis, *Les chrétientés celtiques*, Paris, 1911. Ryan, John, S.J., *Irish Monasticism*, London, 1931. Bury, J. B. *The Life of St. Patrick*, London, 1905. Riguet, *St. Patrice*, Paris, 1911. Martin, E., *St. Colomban (Collection Les Saints)*, Paris, 1905. By the same Colomban (St.) in *Dict. théol.*, col. 370-376. Amann, E., art. Patrice (St.), *Dict. théol.*, col. 2297-2301. Vacandard, E., Vie de St. Bernard, 1894, Paris (Ch. XXIX, St. Malachie O'Morgair, p. 360-388).

[2] Gougaud, p. 63-78.

attracted to the foot of his column, among other foreigners numerous Britons. It is Theodoret of Cyr, who wrote during the lifetime of the Stylite, who tells us this[3].

In 432, when Patrick returned to Ireland with Episcopal power to take the place of Palladius, who had been consecrated by Pope Celestine the previous year, and who died prematurely[4], he undertook a general evangelization, at least in the east, and with a real hierarchy attached to the monasteries[5].

The neophytes were, at the time of their conversion, very much attracted by the appeal of Christ for perfect chastity; the writings of the saint, which for that matter are very concise, bear witness to this for the virgins as for the monks[6].

The development of monachism has to go back to the missionaries who converted the island, and who boldly pressed on the newly-baptized to a total renunciation, an appeal which was followed by a very generous response among the masses. The primitive conditions in which the inhabitants were grouped in clans, furthermore favoured the constitution of monastic cities, which were very simple in their origin, analogous to the clans in certain respects, but obviously with a separation of the sexes. The growths were rapid and prodigious in number as in quality. The great monastic cities appeared from the time of the sixth century.

Clonard, in the centre of the island, was one of the first and the largest monasteries of the country, where it was said more than two thousand religious were grouped together: it was founded about 520 by St. Finnian, who was himself a disciple of St. David at Menevia, in Wales. Another St. Finnian (+ 590 about), of royal race, founded Moville, in the north-east of the island in the sixth century, while St. Enda (or Enna) (+ about 542), who was chief of a tribe, created in the West, in one of the isles of Aran, another centre, the monastery at Killeany, which was also very famous. In the very heart of Ireland, on the Shannon, at Clonmacnois, there rose about the same time one of those monasteries which were called to a most brilliant future, as a home of culture during several centuries: Alcuin, in the IXth century, was in contact with it. However, that which was the most striking from every point of view, was clearly Bangor, situated a little way from Moville to the east of Belfast.

---

[3] *Ibid.,* p. 64-65.

[4] Prosper d'Aquitaine, *Chronique,* a 404. This premature death allows Duchesne to deny the mission of Palladius in Ireland: Hist. anc. de l'Eglise, III, p. 617.

[5] Amann, *o.c.,* col. 2298.

[6] Gougaud, *o.c.,* p. 72-73.

It was founded in 559 by Saint Comgall (or Comgal) and it also counted three thousand monks, evidently divided into sections and very well organized, for work as for prayer. It was from there that the founders of Luxeuil set out with St. Columban.

We must not confound this Saint Columban with St. Columba, who established in Scotland the great monastery of Iona. This Columba (or Columcille) had already founded in Ireland two great monasteries, Derry in the North, and Durrow, when he came to transform the little island of Iona to the West of Scotland, to a real monastic city. It is his glory, and it was to be in fact a headquarters of a lasting and deep evangelization of that country, with a lasting radiance in all that region. The same rôle was to be played in England by the great monastery of Lindisfarne, founded further down in the East, on the North Sea, in the following century by St. Aidan (+ 651). From the sixth century, the monasteries had begun to send to the Continent caravans of missionaries, who bear witness to the vitality of the Christianity of their country, and we must, at least, in a few words, describe their action. The most famous of these missions was that of St. Columban, and it is by this, perhaps, that we know best the truly characteristic features of Irish monachism, if not all its activities[7]. Born in the South-East of Ireland about 540, he responded, from the time of his youth, to the calls to perfection, which were shaking all souls in the country and, after a first monastic initiation, received in another monastery, he came to the great monastery at Bangor whose prestige was then without equal, he knew the founder, Saint Comgall.

In full maturity, about the age of fifty years, he was seized by the mysterious desire for a distant apostolate which was shaking his country. He obtained from Comgall permission to go and evangelize the Germanic people, who were still heathen, with twelve companions, among whom was the future Saint Gall, his nephew. Having called at Great Britain, and having crossed Gaul, he arrived among the Burgundians, where, with the help of the King Gontran, they founded several monasteries, Annegray, Luxeuil and Fontaine.[8]

Luxeuil was the centre of the colony, and it was from there that Columban governed all these little cities. He ruled them with a hand of iron. But his zeal led him to act outside them and nobody escaped from his remonstrances, neither Bishops, nor the neighbouring King, nor the distant Pope.

---

[7] See E. Martin, *op. cit.*, and art. D.T.C., col. 370-374. See also Aigrain, art., Colomban in *Catholicisme*, col. 2297-2301.

[8] Maloury, A., *Quid Luxovienses monachi . . . ad regulam monasteriorum contulerint*, Paris, 1894.

These initiatives, whether they were opportune or imprudent, irritated the aged Queen Brunehaut, who was all-powerful, and she had him expelled in 610. With his Irish companions, he was taken as far as Nantes, with a view to sending him back into his own country; but the group was delivered by a miracle. He resumed his travels, came back towards the East as far as the Rhine, and laid the basis of new foundations. Columban, however, did not stay there; he crossed Switzerland and eventually came to the valley of the Po, occupied by the Lombards, founded Bobbio, which remains the great work of Saint Columban, after Luxeuil. It was there that he died in 615.

This monastic epic remained famous, and for a long time, in the holy island, it had its influence on generous minds and hearts, who were also attracted by the distant apostolate. The monastic cities between the Seine and the Rhine were to be numberless, owing their foundations to similar caravans, which had come from Ireland or Great Britain, in the sixth or the seventh century[9].

II. THE FOUNDATION OF IRISH SPIRITUALITY

The facts as told, small though they are, can help us to characterize the main features of Irish spirituality at the beginning of the Middle Ages. Christian and Catholic, it is evidently identical with all others, but this does not exclude the strong points, which in other regions are less striking. A certain dependence on the primitive forms of Oriental monachism can be seen from the beginning, by the intermediary of the British pilgrims, who after visiting Palestine, pushed on till they reached the holy solitudes.

Another tendency, less fortunate in this case, which also perhaps came from the East, although bound up with the British monk who incarnated it, Palladius, seems also to have had some real but distant influence on Irish spirituality and its origins without falling into heresy with exceptions. This will account for the taste, or to say that passion for ascetic prowess which was so dear to the Scottish monks, but there again we must be careful to stand on our own to stay within the bound of probability and without doubt reality.

The real monastic inspiration is to be found in the words of Christ to the rich young man which made such an impression on St. Anthony of Egypt: " Sell all you have and give to the poor and you will have a treasure in heaven, and come and follow Me " (Luke

---

[9] Gougaud, o.c., C. IV, pp. 134-174.

XVIII-22). The promise of this treasure in heaven was the real source of the monastic vocations in the East and the West. The promise of Christ has no limit within time or space. It raised vocations by the thousand in Ireland as in Africa. Here is the real point of departure of the laws of religious perfection which are inscribed in the monastic rules: " The fundamental principle is that this life is not the true life, and that we must carefully make the best of our hours here below, to prepare for our eternal future. The monk then, that is to say the Christian, who, by a prudent care for the interests of his soul, aspires to total perfection, has to have in view complete detachment. For the simple faithful, to keep clear of sin and its occasions is all that is required; absolute abnegation is the aim of the religious life."[10]

This inspiration is the eminent grace, particularly attributed by theologians to the gift of knowledge which has for its special effect to make known the vanity of created compared to the divine values which besides, thanks to the gift of intelligence, are better entered into, at least in principle.

These effects of the gifts of the Holy Ghost have a mystical character, but they are far from alone constituting mysticism. Rather can one see a distant appeal to this, that authentic appeal of the rest, and how fertile it is! In fact, in spite of its beginnings Irish monachism seems to be much more preoccupied with asceticism than with contemplation, so called, in the personal sense which will be given later.

:-:   :-:   :-:

The Irish monastic rules are scarcely known except by that of Luxeuil, which was manifestly inspired by them, if it was not the original copy. They all share in the principle which must be upheld, in the search for perfection, of the souls which have once undertaken it. Self-denial is above all the road to sanctity: it has been said about Columbanian asceticism: " This fundamental principle is to be found at the base of all monastic codes; that which specially belongs to St. Columban is that he implied it strictly with an energy which is at times disconcerting. His disciple had full liberty to remain in the world; if he wished to be a monk, he must therefore be logical with himself and logical down to the end, and if sometimes his will fails, they will know how to constrain him to take on the bitter and rough paths once again."[11]

We consider the *Regula monachorum* of Luxeuil to be an echo of

---

[10] E. Martin, art. cit., col. 371-372.

[11] *Ibid.* col. 372.

that of Bangor, which has been lost, but which was itself, so it would seem, the synthesis of the best Irish foundations of the sixth century. The three vows of religion sustain the edifice of perfection which is held in view: 1. OBEDIENCE, 2. SILENCE, 3. NOURISHMENT AND FOOD, 4. POVERTY, 5. VANITIES TO BE DESPISED, 6. CHASTITY, 7. THE SINGING OF PSALMS, 8. DISCRETION, 9. MORTIFICATION, 10. THE PERFECTION OF THE MONK, everything is condensed to the full.

The existence of the vows properly so called, of OBEDIENCE, POVERTY and CHASTITY above all have been put in doubt; but this is without any valid reason[12]. These three virtues are from that period solemnly vowed to God. Nuns had their separate monasteries: we have proofs from the beginning of the sixth century[13]. This does not exclude the cases of virgins consecrated to God who persecuted by their family had found protectors in the men of the Church, from whom they took their initiation to this angelic life.

:-:   :-:   :-:

The most striking feature of Irish monachism is its austerity, which has become legendary. We should not, however, insist too much on certain original qualities, which are curious rather than deep, to the detriment of that which is essential. Now, the latter is constituted by the three classic activities, study, to which is added fasting in its various degrees, and certain current practices of asceticism.

Prayer made up every day for most of the monks, the Psalter as a whole or in a notable part usually a third: they generally spoke of three fifties, and several rules imposed them every day. Prayer was also accompanied by prostrations in the Oriental manner. They prayed sometimes with the arms in the form of a cross, sometimes with genuflections: the body thus played a large part in the movement of the soul towards God.

Manual labour was the rule for most of the monks who were not priests. The common occupations were outside guarding the flocks, the crops and beating out the corn; inside that of the artisans and the gold and silver workers, the copyists and the miniaturists; real masterpieces came out of the workshops, improvised at first, but organized little by little.

Intellectual work properly so-called, or study at all its degrees, went on gradually developing, and in fact, the Irish monasteries became famous centres of culture at a period when the work of the

---

[12] Gougaud, o.c., p. 88-89.

[13] Ibid., p. 92-96.

mind was held in little honour on the Continent. The " Scottish " masters enjoyed a favourable reputation, relatively no doubt, but well-deserved at that period. This work was in its way, like manual labour, a prayer the same time as it was as a sacrifice.

Irish asceticism remained celebrated for various practices of austerity of a very local character. The *crosfigill* (vigil of the cross or prayer of the cross) is not only an insistent form of supplication or elevation, but a penance when prolonged, and some monks carried this practice to unimaginable degrees. It has aroused pious legends dear to the Scots. One of them tells how St. Kevin of Glendalough, remained for seven years leaning onto a plank in the position of the *crosfigill*, neither closing an eye by day or by night, and so motionless that the birds made their nests in his hands. Independently of their poetic beauty, these legendary features should be studied. They bear witness in their way to the singular popularity enjoyed by this ancient Christian devotion in the mediaeval Celtic world[14].

The Irish customs of plunging into streams of cold water or ponds that were almost frozen and remaining there a long time while reciting the Psalms, form part of the same preoccupation for uniting penance with prayer. The origin of this has been attributed to St. Patrick. He also added the intention of combating the ardours of concupiscence. The practice was sometimes regulated, at Kil-ros, for example, where the bath was taken more or less conventually after the synaxis. It was imposed as a sanction following on recognized failings. One could thus talk of a *penitential bath* in the full sense of the word[15].

The voluntary deprivation of food is the most common practice of asceticism, and it was evidently observed in Ireland as in the East, in spite of the rigours of the climate. Meat was unknown in the monasteries, and sometimes fish. Eggs were reserved for the feasts and skimmed milk was a luxury drink. In St. Columban's monasteries fasting was perpetual: one simple meal each day before nones or even after nones on Wednesday and Friday. Many of the saints still added personally to these prescriptions of the rule : " Such privations for people living in rough climates of the North are a heroism which stupefies."[16]

:-:   :-:   :-:

If we now look at the deep spirit of monachism, we shall certainly

---

[14] *Ibid.*, pp. 99-100.

[15] See Dom Gougaud, *La mortification pa les bains froids*, in *Bull. d'anc. Litt. et d'Archéologie chrét.*, 1914, pp. 96-108.

[16] Gougaud, *o.c.*, p. 103.

find a tendency towards the contemplative life, in the canonical
recitation of the office. This without a doubt shows certain modalities
but these are secondary. Certain Psalms were cut by collects, if not
all of them, in the common Oriental fashion. The ancient Irish liturgy
does not shine with originality, rather should we speak of eclecticism
and even, in a picturesque fashion, of " patchwork ".[17]

All this was an echo of the East. On the other hand, prayer, in
the form of a litany which was called *lorica,* has a special quality
of its own, and perhaps we shall find a mystical note in these
repetitions and accumulations of antitheses which fix the soul in a
superior ideal, in spite of the multiplied details which could make
the soul heavy, but which could also lift it towards God : " These
long enumerations of petitions, these series of adjurations, ardent
invocations, these enumerations of spiritual and bodily dangers . . .
the whole, divided by pious aspirations, pressing effusions towards
God and the Saints, strong sentiments of repentance, compunction,
of distrust of self, that is what gives to these ancient Celtic prayers
an appearance and a very special quality."[18]

The spirit of contemplation which the call to the monastery contained in germ and of which the life of the monk kept the ardour
found its completion in the great retreat that certain of the ancients
managed to achieve, whether in some solitary island exposed to the
attacks of pirates, or at least in isolated places, beneath the rocks in
peaceful grottos favourable for prayer : " The desert in Ireland, the
peniti of our Brittany responded to the needs of these retreatants.
The great number of names of Irish places, in the composition of
which the word *disert* plays a part, shows how much eremitical habits
were in favour in that country. Many saints from 559 to 665,
sanctified themselves in solitude."[19]

According to the documents known up to now, Irish monachism
was dominated as a whole by asceticism rather than mysticism. We
are far here from the contemplative tendencies which characterize the
Eastern spiritual centres and even many of the Western ones at the
time of the Fathers. The doctrinal note was dominant with them,
frankly turned, at least among the masters, towards the contemplation
of the highest mysteries : The Holy Trinity, Christ, Grace, The
Church. In the Irish tradition, we do not find anything analogous
to the profound spiritual institutions of a St. Ephrem or a Cassian,
of a St. Basil or a St. Gregory, of a St. John Chrysostom or a St.
Augustine, not even of a St. Gregory the Great who was however,

---

[17] E. Bishop, *Journal of Theological Studies,* 1907, p. 279.
[18] Gougaud, *o.c.,* pp. 312-313.
[19] *Ibid.,* p. 104.

as Pope, given over to action. Asceticism clearly dominates Irish
spirituality at the highest period, that which flowered among many
of them into missionary journeys, when these were not merely an
escape; this is not excluded, but could not be taken for a common
rule without injustice: the work of these apostles has proved the
value of the spirit which led them as a whole.

III.   ZENITH, DECADENCE, REVIVAL

The sixth and the seventh centuries were a zenith for the Scottish
islanders. "The Monasteries multiplied and the number of their
inhabitants increased to an extraordinary extent. The Christian Life,
the ascetic Life, the spirit of conversion developed to a marvellous
degree. From neighbouring countries people came to be formed in
the perfect life, and also to learn the profane and sacred sciences,
for it was in this island, situated on the confines of the inhabited
world, that learning took refuge, surrounded as it was on all sides
by barbarism."[20]

This prosperity was very radiant in the eighth century, when the
Irish monks came to the Continent in imposing numbers, founding
abbeys, and working for the evangelization of Western Europe. Their
action furthermore was not exclusively religious. The monasteries
had become brilliant centres of literary culture, specially Latin, certainly a relative culture but interesting for the period. So modest
was the movement of study which was aroused by Charlemagne, and
which attracted into the Frankish countries men of letters from beyond
the sea, such as Alcuin, and which continued after the great emperor.
Ireland was represented by a genius who was, unfortunately, imperfectly balanced, John Scotus Eriugena, who showed an astonishing
aptitude at making syntheses, audacious and premature though they
were, notably in philosophy. The religious spirit had not sufficiently
prepared his soul and the others for such a high enterprise. The
work was brilliant but it lacked in depth; thence came its main dangers.
There were others besides[21].

In spite of its radiant prosperity, Irish Christianity, of which
monachism was the soul, bore in its bosom the germs of weakness.
Do not let us insist too much on the disciplinary controversies, as
if there was here a latent schism: "That this Church has kept for
a long time, in the bosom of a great Catholic unity, an original

[20] *Ibid.*, p. 347.
[21] Vernet, F. Erigène, in *Dict. théol. cath.*, col. 401-434.

appearance, a little in retreat and in the shadows, is clear; but to claim that she showed any proof of hostile sentiments, or even of defiance, or even indifference in regard to the Mother Church of Christianity, this is frankly in disagreement with our best sources of information."[22]

The cause of the evil was more the absence of a true hierarchy outside the monasteries, for the work undertaken by St. Patrick in this regard was not lasting. Later, the radiant power of the abbeys was not enough to assure a solid organization of religious and sacerdotal activities. The missionary spirit itself needed to be tempered, for there was much natural ardour in this desire to be expatriated, if one must thus translate the remark[23] of a great monk of the ninth century, Walafrid Strabon: *Quibus consuetudo peregrinandi jam pene in naturam conversa est*[24]. Thence came a number of abuses in what might be described as the "losses of emigration" [25].

The true causes of the decadence came, above all, from without; there were the Norman and Danish invasions, which ravaged Ireland like all the Western countries of Europe. Feudalism and its perpetual struggles even reached the clerics; for the Church was deprived of all real independence and all effective authority. Thence the spiritual decadence which historians deplore, aggravated by a certain practical independence, which was not a separation from Rome, but an "insular isolation", favouring the policy of letting be.

There was a certain improvement at the end of the twelfth century, under the influence of the Archbishops of Canterbury, of whom those of Ireland were the suffragans, notably since the time of St. Anselm. The best bishops of Ireland were in favour of this movement, in particular Gilebert of Limerick, who was even named as legate of the Holy See in Ireland. But the most famous of the reformers of the country was St. Malachy (1094-1148), the friend of St. Bernard, who received him several times at Clairvaux, and who consecrated to him a very moving tribute, after his death, which took place in this monastery, in the course of his journey *ad limina*.

The Cistercians were, indeed, the instruments of providence in this work of monastic reform. It has been believed for a long time that the Benedictine rule had been adopted in the Irish monasteries of the seventh or eighth centuries, as in those of the Continent

---

[22] Gougaud, *o.c.*, p. 209.

[23] See Dom Gougaud, *o.c.*, p. 348.

[24] *Vita Sancti Galli*, II, 41.

[25] Gougaud, *o.c.*, pp. 153-160.

from the seventh or the eighth century; Mabillon himself thought so, but this is an error thinks Dom Gougaud: " The rule of St. Benedict was certainly known literally in Ireland, in the seventh and eighth centuries, but that it became law in the Irish monasteries before the arrival of the Cistercians, is a thing that no documents will allow us to affirm."[26] In fact St. Bernard saw six Cistercian abbeys opened in Ireland which contributed most effectively to the reform of the clergy.

A contemporary historian offers his homage to the piety, to the chastity, to the personal virtues of the clergy that the reform had touched[27]. He reproaches them, however, for having confined themselves too narrowly under the eye of the Bishop or of the Abbot, in solitude and the exercises of the cloister and to have neglected the instruction of the people who were without the advice that all the influences produce."[28] This work Malachy was not able to complete and " the Cistercians whom he had called to his aid were themselves incapable of completing it," writes Vacandard. They had at least the merit of undertaking the serious work in its full depth.

St. Bernard had an intuition of this, and in order to show it he drew a very dark picture of the condition of the island: " Order succeeds anarchy, the catholic home is born again, agriculture flourishes once more, intellectual activity sets to work. The religious life, established once more in the monasteries, is the soul of all this progress."[29] This ideal has evidently never been achieved and the work has never been completed. The Cistercians had at least declared it in spreading " around them religious instruction and a taste for agriculture. In that regard nobody rendered greater services to Ireland, and if the Abbot of Clairvaux had been able to read into the future it would have been a consolation for him to think that he had contributed on his part to the making of the people hardworking and strong who later would have to suffer so much for their faith.[30] All these united influences gave to the Irish people its profound religious vitality from ancient times, and prepared that spirit of the apostolate which remains today one of the fruits and riches of this Christian and apostolic life.

---

[26] *Ibid.*, p. 365.
[27] Vacandard, *o.c.*, II, p. 374.
[28] *Ibid.*, p. 375.
[29] *Ibid.*, p. 388.
[30] *Ibid.*, p. 374.

The Irish Penitentials

By GABRIEL LE BRAS,

Professor of the Faculty of Law at the University of Paris

IN the centuries when Mediaeval Christianity was born—between the fall of the Empire and the end of the Carolingian dynasty—the original and surprising literature of the penitentials invaded the West[1]. These tariffs of punishments applicable to every type of sin, came from the isles of the North, first Ireland, and Wales[2]. There is a ladder of failings and faults and of penalties, which bear witness to the social and moral state of a people who were still half pagan and for whom the apostle monks dreamt of an ascetic ideal[3]. The importance surpasses the local scene by a long way; it is the practice of a sacrament which they set out to regulate[4]. A prodigious missionary activity implanted this conception in all the West. The sketch of the outer development of the content of the bearing of these Irish penitentials will make more intelligible for us the part of the Celt in the history of civilization.

:-:   :-:   :-:

Patrick was the precursor. Under his authority the canons of two synods were transmitted, of which a second resembled more the biblical justification of disciplinary rules or, if you prefer, the canon

---

[1] There is a general account, with a bibliography in Paul Fournier and Gabriel le Bras, *Histoire des collections canoniques en Occident*, t. I., 1931, pp. 50-62, 90-91, 98, 99, 108-112, 347-356, and in our article *Penitentiels* in *Dictionnaire de Théologie Catholique*. Since 1931 some studies have appeared to which we will draw attention at the right time. John T. McNeill (one of the most learned men as regards the system) has given with the aid of Elena M. Gamer, *Die Bussordnungen der abendlandischen Kirche* . . . 1851, and H. J. Schmitz, *Die Bussbucher and die Bussdisciplin der Kirche*, t. I, 1883; t. II, 1898. We shall designate these two collections by the letters W. & S. In our article *Penitentiels* will be found the histories of these publications, since the XVIth century.

[2] See the collection of these forms of Christianity in the solid works of Dom Gougaud. *Les Chrétientés Celtiques*, 2nd ed., 1911, can be consulted with profit.

[3] Rev. J. Ryan, S.J., *Irish Monasticism: Origins and Early Development*, Dublin and Cork, 1931. Fr. Ryan, who is professor at University College, Dublin, is a master of studies on Celtic origins in Ireland: I had the good fortune to receive his instructions at Glendalough and elsewhere.

[4] To put our subject in a theological framework, it will be enough to read the article *Pénitence* in *Dictionnaire de Théologie Catholique*.

law taken from the Sacred Scriptures, while the first already formu-
lates some penalties[5]. The most ancient of the genuine penitentials
is that of a certain Finnian, whom everything points to identifying
with the lettered monk who was a companion of Gildas, of David
and of Cadoc, and died about 550. It is in this Welsh-Irish circle
that the system took on a final definite form. Two synods of uncertain
date, two works attributed to David and Gildas, seem to belong to
Wales[6], while Finnian, settled in the monastery at Clonard, was
preparing a catalogue of penalties applicable to clerics and to the
laity with fine discriminations[7]. A manual of direction, another of
repression, was offered to all the Irish clergy for spiritual conversion.

Why did this literature come to birth in Celtic countries ? In the
need for an exomologesis of this ardent people who were haunted
by perspectives of the world beyond; the custom of confession in
the monasteries, which formed the only ecclesiastical structure of
Christianity in the territorial hierarchy; the secular custom of redeeming private sins; ignorance of the ancient procedures for public
penance: all these are explanations of an original practice in the
Church, although it was not without its analogies in other religious
societies[8].

Towards the end of the sixth century, the system was introduced
on the Continent. According to all appearance, Columban composed
in the region of Luxeuil his bi-partite penitential in which are en-
visaged successively the faults of monks and those of laiety[9]. Of the
twenty-five canons of the second part, fourteen were inspired by
Finnian; the influence of David can be felt even more than that
of Gildas, whose sanctions Columban accentuates.

It is on the contrary under a continental influence, that of Cassian,
that Cummean composed in Ireland (there is every reason for
believing this), the penitential of which the original text was only

---

[5] Edited by Haddan and Stubbs. See L. Bieler, *The Works of St.
Patrick*, London, 1953 (in this will be found the translation of the 34 canons
of the first synod and a good bibliography).

[6] All these texts are in W., S., Haddan and Stubbs have also inserted them.

[7] Editions W. and S. Three manuscripts of the IXth century, one of the
Xth century.

[8] The comparisons with India naturally present themselves to the mind,
and they have aroused various reflections.

[9] The best edition is that of O. Seebass in *Zeitschr. fur Kirchengesch.*,
XIV (1894) offer the two remaining manuscripts, of the Xth and XIth centuries, originating at Bobbio and preserved in the National Library of
Turin. At the International Congress of Luxeuil (1950) there were presented two communications by G. Mitchell and A. Bergamaschi, on this
penitential. They can be read in the *Mélanges Colombaniens*, Paris (Alsatia),
1951, pp. 143-151 and 155-163.

discovered in the twentieth century[10]. Following the order of his model he fixes the punishment of capital sins and of minor sins. All the penitentials drawn up in Ireland have been made use of in this summa which crowns the series.

Two manuscripts of the National Library in Paris, preserve an enigmatic collection, which has been called *Canones hibernenses*, formed of six separate pieces of which the first (Irish synod and discourse of Gregory of Nazianzus) sets out twenty-five canons on homicide, the sins of the flesh, food; the third only concerns the wounds given to Bishops and priests (Irish synod: eight canons); the fourth, the refusal of hospitality to clerics (prologue and six canons). Neither the date of each part, nor that of the collection as a whole, seems to us to be assured: one may admit a secular arrangement, or a compilation more or less contemporary of the work of Cummean[11].

The authors of penitentials invoke unexceptionable authorities, whether the Scriptures or National Synods[12]. Other sources as pure as these are to be found, the councils and the Fathers, and their doctrine does not lend much to criticism. That which can awake criticism is the absence of precision as to the synods which are invoked, the actual value of the scriptural deductions, the arbitrary fixing of tariffs and the transference to relationships with God, of a system of legal compilations.

At the end of the seventh century, the creative force was worn out, but the ancient collections would be copiously used. Certain works emerge directly from them and the penitentials of the diverse Churches, certain canonical collections borrow some elements from them.

Seven penitentials of the seventh century and of the first half of the eighth are taken in whole or in part from Columbanian sources and lack, almost all of them, the slightest originality.[13] The diverse Celtic penitentials went to the making of the celebrated

---

[10] According to Zettinger, who published it in *Archiv fur Kath. Kirchen-recht*, LXXXII (1902), pp. 501-540. Account by McNeill-Gamer, pp. 98-99. One of our Polish students, Edouard Blericq, has presented a thesis which has remained in manuscript on this penitential.

[11] Edit. according to the Latin manuscripts 3182 and 12021, of the National Library in Paris, which are the only ones that survive.

[12] No synod has a date. The scriptures are sometimes quoted, sometimes understood.

[13] Edited after classification by W.

Anglo-Saxon penitentials of the Theodorian families[14]. And the double ascendancy—Irish and English—is to be found in the *Bigotianum* and the *Gwynnanium,* finally in the *Excarpsus Cummeani* which have, for a long time, passed for the original work of Cummean which had in the Middle Age the greatest diffusion[15]. Also clear is the Irish presence in the English penitentials but under the name of Bede or Egbert, and in the " Spanish " penitentials at the end of the eighth century: *Albeldense* and *Silense*[16]. It is specially denounced in the tripartite contemporaries which were composed by the Frankish clergy and where Columban and Cummean reigned alongside Theodore: *Sangallense tripartitum, Capitula judicorum*[17].

Nobody will be astonished at the welcome given to the Celtic penitentials by the Irish collection, *Hibernensis,* which was to exercise in the eighth century such a widespread influence[18]. By this means, as much as by the original documents, was spread the insular system when the Carolingian reaction burst out.

:-:   :-:   :-:

The Carolingian reform attempted a return to ancient customs which included public penance and a restoration of hierarchical authority. Now the penitentials represent an invention which was late and local. Hostility in their regard was late to show itself. In the second half of the eighth century, it seems they limited themselves to a choice, and the selections which we have pointed out give

---

[14] The notices of McNeill-Gamer resume the discussions, in which they have taken part, around the edition given by Finsterwalder, *Die canones Theodori Cantuariensis unde ihre Ueberlieferungsformen, Weimar,* 1929. What interests us in a special way, is the use of certain Irish sources.

[15] The manuscript of the Bigot collection, National Library of Paris, lat. 3182 edited W. & S., we call *Gwynnianum,* to render homage to a learned man, and for convenience, the collection in ancient Irish edited by E. J. Gwynn with a translation in *Eriu,* VII (1914). The *Excarpsus Cummeani,* edited by W. & S. which was for a long time regarded as a true *Cummean,* mingles Theodorian fragments or *Colombanian* ones to *Cummean,* his principal model.

[16] F. Romero-Otazo has published a new edition of the manuscript of *Alveldencse* (or *Vigilanum*) which is reserved at the Escurial, and has distributed some photo-copies of the manuscript in the British Museum which keeps for us the *Silense.* These two collections, which are closely related, have been fed by the insular canons, as I have had occasion to show. On this series placed under the patronage of Bede and Egbert, turn to the accounts of McNeill-Gamer.

[17] Edit. W. & S.

[18] Wasserchleben, *Die irische Kanonensammlung,* 2nd edition, 1885, and in regard to this collection, the *Histoire des collections canoniques,* t. I, pp. 62-64, and the note of McNeill-Gamer.

the best part to Irishmen[19]. But at the beginning of the ninth century, a revolt exploded. The Council of Chalons (813) ordered the total elimination of the books known as penitentials " of which the errors are as certain as the authors are uncertain ". And the Council of Paris (829), directed that they should be burned as anti-canonical. The Archbishops criticized them in no uncertain terms and the Irish enterprise, which for so long was fortunate, seemed to be destined to disaster[20].

This was pure illusion! As confession had not been abolished tariffs remained necessary. When Ebbon, the Archbishop of Bourges, begged Halitgaire to compose a new manual, the Bishop of Cambrai drew from Columban and Cummean (also from Theodore) all that agreed with Roman discipline[21]. Between 830 and 847, a French cleric drew from the main sources the elements of a pseudo-Theodore, of which the success was considerable[22].

Between 850 and 1000, the success of the tripartites redoubled. According to the Roman etiquette, which Halitgaire had already usurped (and which Mgr. Schmitz was to attempt with enthusiasm on account of his passionate ultramontanism), a *Cassinense* took from the *Capitula judiciorum* four-fifths of its texts; under the patronage invented by Gregory III, Cummean spread himself out; a manuscript of the Ambrosian revived the old gall.[23]

A little after the year 1000, the canonical collections were opened for the second time to the penitentials. Cummean furnished to Burchard's *decret* thirty canons and a Collection in V books borrowed from the *Capitula judiciorum*[24].

A second reaction was near. As violent as the Carolingian re-formers, the Gregorians set on to the authors of the penitentials, men sunk in vices, who polluted, with their falsified products, the holy ordinance of the laws. Peter Damien throws them into the

---

[19] We have pointed out the passage and without exhausting the list of collections which attest this influence : *Remense,* or *Burgundense,* for example.

[20] As regards all this reaction see *Histoire des collections canoniques,* t. I, pp. 98-100.

[21] Edit. W. & S. The proof of the borrowing from the islanders has been furnished by Paul Fournier, who identifies three series : canonical and Columbanian (c. 1-54), Celtic (c. 55-77), Theodorian (c. 78-104).

[22] Edit. W.

[23] *Article Pénitentiels,* col. 1174-1175. Mgr. Schmitz, obsessed with the conviction of a Roman origin of the penitentials, has drawn up an argument from the Roman etiquette of which the parents are, Halitgaire, the *Cassinense* and pseudo-Gregory.

[24] Paul Fournier counted fifteen texts of Cummean and thirteen of the *Excarpsus Cummeani* in the *Decret* of Burchard.

fire of Gomorrah, while Atton limits himself to unmasking them[25]. However, the *Capitula judiciorum* are to be found among the sources of the most famous of the Gregorian canonists, Anselm of Lucca and Bonizo de Sutri will be debtors of Cummean[26]. Burchard's *Decret* was to set the tone of the collections and notably the *Decret* of Ivo of Chartres[27].

About 1140, Gratian's *Concordia,* the last of the canonical collections, and the first setting of the *Corpus juris canonici* was to welcome under inscriptions which give no suspicion of their origin the rare texts of the Celtic penitentials[28]. If he was unaware of the manuscripts of the creators, it was their work which he honoured, transmitted by numerous intermediaries, of whom pseudo-Theodore and Ivo of Chartres were the most effectual.

Down to the end of the Middle Ages, the decretalists commented in the universities on some texts of Columban and Cummean which had become anonymous[29]. This Celtic matter enters into modern doctrine, then into the *Codex* of 1917: no longer by the adaptation of texts which had been forgotten for a long time (and which the learned men of today are discovering once again) but by a consecration of principles and procedures which we must now bring out[30].

:-:   :-:   :-:

Sins, penalties, the application of the penalty to the sin; the penitentials give the whole Celtic conception of internal order and social policy. The Irish did not invent a classification of sins[31]. One can recognize in the first penitentials the three unpardonable sins of the primitive Church, idolatry, fornication and homicide. Cummean adopted a series of eight, and had it adopted: gluttony, luxuria, cupidity, anger, melancholy, accidie, boasting and pride to which he added peccadilloes (*minutiae causae*) and specially certain fallings-

---

[25] *Histoire des collections canoniques* . . . t. II, pp. 6-7.

[26] pp. 29-30 and p. 143. What Anselm borrowed from the Irishman is, in fact, very little.

[27] Again a moderate borrowing. The *Panormie* sets aside the penitential texts.

[28] Research should be conducted methodically, and the *Prolegomenas of* Friedberg will scarcely any help for a harvest which would be very small. Of the *De consecratione,* dist. II, c. 27-94, the Cummeanian descent is recognised.

[29] The ordinary gloss of the two texts quoted in the previous note is completely theological.

[30] The texts became progressively effaced, in proportion, as their substance became incorporated in the common law.

[31] However, efforts were sustained in the Cummeanian lineage, for example by the author of *Bigotianum.*

off in discipline[32]. A general classifying would raise us from the coarseness of archaic performances to the refinements of Christian psychoanalysis.

The list of pagan practices puts us in the presence of a world haunted by bogeys and bounded by taboos. Belief in vampires, in werewolves, consultations of soothsayers and omens, funeral incantations, absorption of the blood or urine of an animal, or of a liquid drawn from a fox, a crow, a cock or a hen.[33] If pagan customs are forbidden, certain authors demand the application of the Biblical taboos (which no longer had, however, the ancient justifications): Adamnan makes the prohibitions of Exodus and Leviticus live once more[34]. " Whether cooked or raw, reject that which has been contaminated by a leech." While the contamination of pork does not exclude its cooking as a food, which will be absorbed by the impure.

These prescriptions which remain so close to the material, are allied with the most spiritual concerns. Finnian begins his penitential with an analysis of the combats of the flesh and of thought, discerning the passing temptation, the hesitations, the intentions, the want of attention.

In the chapter on sexual grossness, the penitentials rival each other in their elaboration: adultery, incest, bestiality, sodomy, and all the ingenuity or abomination of these diverse aberrations file past in long lists that one hesitates to translate[35]. Blows and wounds, excess at table, perjury and false witness lead to precise but less subtle definitions.

Under the rubric of diverse sins, many combinations can take place. Thus Cummean links perjury with avarice and blasphemy with envy.[36] Among the misdeeds of gluttony the Gwynnianum ranks lack of cleanliness. " One hundred strokes on the dirty hands and forty days of penance for the cook who lets something dirty or discolouring fall into a liquid."

The authors of penitentials have laid down catalogues of sins which leave no serious failings in the shade. They are less careful about formal logic than about effective punishment; a glance at the penalties will show this.

:-:   :-:   :-:

The first aim of penance has always been the healing of the soul,

---

[32] Third series: light faults, children's offences, respect for sacred things.
[33] *Canones hibernenses*, first series.
[34] Edit. Haddan and Stubbs. (*Councils*, II).
[35] Dr. Gwynn has preferred to translate into Latin rather than English the manifestations of luxuria.
[36] The composition of each group is worthy of study, but the whole of the penitential literature should be studied.

and it has been inspired by a principle of medicine in antiquity, the radical opposition of the remedy to the disease. *Contraria contrariis sanantur.* By this maxim Finnian justified the imposition on a covetous cleric of the giving of abundant alms, while Columban reduced the chatterer to silence, and the glutton to a fast. Cummean wished to overcome the lazy with work, and condemned the unstable to a sedentary life. What had they in view ? To restore the vital balance, spiritual health[37].

This individual cure is not enough to ensure justice towards God and towards the neighbour. The idea of reparation for harm done expresses itself in the restoration of stolen objects; the idea of a divine reconciliation by prayers, sacrifices, almsgiving.

Every offence against God calls for a punishment. Although its vindictive character remains in the second place, it is implied by natural reason and positive discipline. Remedy, reparation, punishment; most of these penalties have this triple object in view. A summary examination of each category will make clear their value on many sides.

The nature of the penalties is as complex as their object. However, we can distinguish (without separating them) devotions, asceticism, terms of settlement.

There is no devotion more familiar to monks than the singing of psalms. Cummean imposes this on those who give ill-timed snubs, on the tellers of idle tales, and those guilty of deceptions by night[38].

The most usual penalty was the privation of food, which could vary from partial abstinence to a complete fast. A conversation alone with a woman entailed the loss of dinner; the taking of a liquid soiled by a domestic animal, or eating a meal in a place sacred to paganism meant forty days on bread and water; the secret fornication of a priest was punished with a year on bread and water and two years' abstinence from meat and wine. The best adapted of these privations are in the chapter on gluttony[39].

Columban is not sparing in blows, nor the Gwynnianum which lays down a hundred strokes with a strap on the hands of whoever, in good faith and without causing harm, bears false witness against his neighbour; if he is in bad faith, seven hundred strokes with a whip, combined with a semi-fast and a hundred and fifty psalms[40].

---

[37] McNeill-Gamer, p. 44.
[38] There is an enumeration of the psalms prescribed at the end of the table published by Kuno Meyer.
[39] Here are some of Cummean's sanctions, ch. I: distension of the stomach: one day's penance; vomiting: seven days; excess of wine or beer: seven days; to inebriate a companion out of good nature: the same penalties.
[40] Chap. III, c. 17.

Penalties imitated from civil custom were added on, and were sometimes substituted for the canonical penalties: pecuniary settlement and exile. Whoever has inflicted a bleeding wound on the Bishop must pay the value of seven female slaves; if the blood does not run down to the ground, then it is half the tariff, unless he prefers to let his hand be cut off[41]. Columban requires from the seducer that he should pay to the parents the price of his conquest, while Finnian makes the fornicator pay a fine for the redemption of his soul.

Exile is the punishment for the highly guilty; the cleric who kills his neighbour is to be exiled for ten years, the man guilty of incest is condemned to eternal pilgrimage, and it has been supposed that many of those *peregrini* who were wandering about Gaul, during the Frankish period, were penitents.

:-:   :-:   :-:

The penalty is calculated with an apparent rigidity, but applied with a certain suppleness. It is proportioned to the fault according to the weights and measures of the authors. Its weight or its lightness signifies the sentiment of horror which each of them inspired. A patient study of the correspondences would reveal the moral conscience of the ancient Irish.

Great attention is paid to aggravating or attenuating circumstances, to the degree of will on the part of the guilty man, to the repetition of the acts. The place of the guilty man and of the victim in the Christian society determines the severity of the punishment: the lay man is less struck at and less protected than the cleric and the ladder of penalties is the ladder of the hierarchy.

At first sight, this is a mechanical conception of reparation. For a stolen sheep, four sheep will be restored; for an ox, five oxen; for a pig, two pigs. For a horse seized from a Bishop, the guilty person will owe twelve horses[42].

The rigidity of the system is partly attenuated by the conditions of its exercize. To begin with, the penitentials offer a sufficient variety of punishments, and the penitent himself sometimes has an option. The confessor keeps a certain liberty of judgment, and *discretio*, which means an intelligent equity, is recommended to him[43]. Finally, in good time, the tariffs for redemption were worked out; a legal penalty could be replaced by a shorter and a harsher penalty, known

---

[41] *Canones Hibernenses*, third series, c. 1 and 4.

[42] Gwynnianum, ch. III, c. 3; *Canones Hibernenses*, 3rd series, :

[43] The prologues are applied to this, and wise counsels smooth over the enumeration of penalties.

as an *arreum*. This is one of the strangest novelties. It appears in the *Canones hibernenses*, of which the third series is a table of equivalences and another table, of a rather later date, has been preserved for us.[44] A year of penance could be replaced by three days retreat in the sepulchre of a saint, taken up with prayer and the singing of psalms without food or sleep; the *Canones hibernenses* propose this arrangement and six others equally gentle. In the *arrea* published by Kuno Meyer corporal penalties—repeated genuflections, arms in the form of a cross—are combined with long abstinences and the singing of psalms[45].

The penitentials thus constitute a complete system for the repression of all sins. Does not their range surpass all appearances, all practices and techniques? Such is the problem which we must now face.

The historical importance of the Irish penitentials surpassed by a long way that of simple tariffs of expiation. They are witnesses and regulators of the structure and the customs of Ireland; they hold in the evolution of penance a role with a universal range; they respond to a practical conception of relations with God.

To what extent do they give us information about the customs of Irish society or about the imaginations of its spiritual directors ? It is necessary to have integral knowledge of the legacy of paganism, the literary tradition, the formation of the religious, the methods of reasoning and the profound aims in order to appreciate this mass of decisions so full of strangeness. We know that magic survived but in what proportion ? What texts were transmitted, but with what persistent realism? Columban and all the authors had received a training in which the Roman and the insular were mingled, but what sort of mixture did they make of their experience and their inventions ?

It is easier to see their precepts and their ideal. They firmly held the doctrine of the indissolubility of marriage, and this was to be their chief divergence from the Theodorians, who admitted reasons for divorce[46]. In checking sins, which were also misdemeanours or crimes, they supported the secular law[47].

---

[44] Published by Kuno Meyer in the *Revue celtique*, XV, 1894.

[45] It is one of the points of comparison with the practices of India.

[46] We have pointed them out in *l'Histoire des collections canoniques*. Other options, such as the reiteration of baptism, offended the Romans. The indissolubility of marriage was clearly affirmed by the Irish, from the time of Finnian's penitential.

[47] Oakley, to whom we owe so much fine work on the penitentials, has specially studied this co-operation of the two laws.

In many ways they increase the demands of the common law. By their prohibitions and restrictions as regards food, they discipline the diet. By their calendar of married relations, they impose a continence which is scarcely interrupted for the sake of procreation[48].

If nothing authorizes us to consider the picture of the vices which they punish as a portrait of Irish social life, we have every reason to believe that the vigorous policy of the Church raised the moral level of the Christians.

:-:   :-:   :-:

Far from being confined to Ireland, the penitentials reached the whole of Western Christianity, and the gravest problem they set before us is a oecumenical problem, belonging to the history of theology : what, in the development of penance, is the role of the Irish penitentials ? For the sinners of the first centuries, a public penance was prescribed with a view to their conversion; the Bishop took them back into the community, after a period as penitents, which could not be renewed in the case of a second fall. The Irish system organized a penance which could be private, which never placed the penitent in a separate group, and which could be repeated after each sin. It is for the historians of theology to recognize in antiquity the attraction of these characteristics[49]. Our business is to record the part played by each of the three elements of penance in the Irish system.

The most striking is, without doubt, that of satisfaction: the object of the penitential is to determine the extent. By asceticism or prayer, the penitent obtains the pardon, not only of the Church but of God. He expiates, he redeems his fault.

A confessor is the intermediary and his function is not the object of treatises; it appears to us in incidents. Though we knew examples in Ireland of confession to laymen, there can be no doubt that the ordinary minister was a priest or a monk. Columban sets out that he is addressing himself to a priest and the preface of the Tripartite of St. Gall even forbids the laity to own a penitential! Better than

---

[48] " Marriage without continence is not lawful, it is guilty . . . God has only allowed the union of the sexes for procreation . . . married couples must abstain from sexual relations for three periods of forty days, then for periods agreed among themselves, the nights of Saturday and Sunday, and during pregnancy." (Finnian, c. 46.)

[49] See, for example, the works of Father Galtier. In two articles in the *Revue d'histoire ecclésiastique*, t. XXXIII, 1937, he studies the transition from Latin to Celtic penance. The same problem is dealt with by Cyrille Vogel, *La discipline pénitentielle en Gaule des origines à la fin du VIIe siècle*, Paris, 1952.

a minister he is a " friend of the soul ", the *anmchara* of the *Senchus Mor*, whom we will readily regard as the doctor or director always attentive to the state of his fallible client[50].

After every fall (and not at certain stated dates), Cummean gives him twelve methods of obtaining remission. The fifth is confession, of which the secret must be scrupulously kept[51]. To reconcile the sinner with God, the priest imposes his hands, as in the traditional practice of the sacrament.

The acts of penance must be accompanied with regret for the sin. Finnian demands devotion of the heart and the table edited by Kuno Meyer insists on the necessity of repentance[52]. " God turns away from hearts in which there is no humble contrition," declares the prologue to the *Bigotianum*.

:-: :-: :-:

The Irish system of private penance had repercussions well beyond the sacramental domain. In relations with God it accentuated the sentiment of an effective conversation; there is neither contract nor constraint, for the Church excludes as radically the idea of a God who is a creditor or a debtor as that of a God directed by magical operations; but there is a divine granting of pardon, following on therapeutic and redeeming sacrifices, accompanied by a request and a conversion.

Public penance also subordinated pardon to regular exercizes. It had none of that elasticity, that familiarity, which the computations bore at its extreme point. From now on, minds would be prepared for all the disciplinary developments which would interpret the concept of the close relation between the Christian and God, the dispenser of graces in exchange for sacrifices. Private Masses and indulgences are not the consequences of the one penitential system; but the profound thought is unique and the Irish followed by the English and the Continentals, have smoothed out one of the chief forms of veneration[53].

The repercussions of their initiative on the structure of the Church, which were more indirect, were also effective. In former times the

---

[50] Another subject for comparison with the customs of India.

[51] B. Kurtscheid, *Das Beichtsiegel in seiner geschicktlichen Entwicklung*, Freiburg-in-Breisgau, 1912.

[52] *Per studium diligentius cordis et corporis*, as St. Finnian states precisely.

[53] N. Paulus gives proofs which we have quoted and developed in the *Revue des Sciences religieuses*, 1925. One can see at the *de arreis* how far the faculty for the redeeming of souls went.

Bishop presided over the acts of public penance. Every priest could now administer private penance and he had the penitential in his hands as a sign of autonomy. He could also be the purveyor of temporal goods. Several penitentials provide for a sort of remuneration of the confessor, and the alms have increased the ecclesiastical fortune (besides that the *Canones hibernes* contain a series on the tithe)[54].

:-:   :-:   :-:

By certain arbitrary qualities, the system of penitentials has caused some trouble in the West. No doubt the authors sometimes defend themselves for following their fancies: but the predecessors whom they invoke remain nameless and unqualified. Each one fixing the tariff of faults according to tradition or his own reckoning, discordances are inevitable and disproportions are disquieting[55].

Because they call for delicacy in the psychology of sin as in the choice of the penalty, the penitentials serve for the education of the cleric as of the faithful. They inspire them with a sense of material cleanliness as of moral purity. The justice of men draws as much profit from them as the justice of God[56].

As initiators of the penitentials, respectful of principles, ingenious in application, the Irish have contributed more than any other people in the dark ages to the progress of the moral conscience in the West.

---

[54] Thus, those alleged by the author of the *Bigotianum*.

[55] There are examples in the *Histoire des collections canoniques*, pp. 59 and 89.

[56] We have developed this eulogy in the above work, pp. 56-57, and it has been ratified by good judges.

The Contribution of Ireland to Medieval Christian Thought

By MGR. RENÉ AIGRAM

IN the works of Alcuin, the celebrated Englishman, who under Charlemagne became the chief light in the Palatine school, there is a letter addressed " to the Brothers who in the Isle of Ireland devoted themselves in various places to the service of God "; in this remarkable epistle, in which we might say in modern terms that he sketches out a science of teaching of profane letters oriented towards a study of the sacred Scriptures, Alcuin makes a fine eulogy of the " three learned Irish masters, who were responsible for such great progress in the Christian churches in Brittany, Gaul and in Italy ". In thus expressing himself, it is clear that this master, who was universally admired in his generation, intended to pay a debt of gratitude; it was far, however, from being merely personal to himself, as the Doctor was already teaching that the Venerable Bede had with insistence given a similar homage to the Irish; sometimes he speaks of the Irish, or the Scotti, who were coming over to England and had become the teachers of the youth of England, forming them at the same time in serious studies, *Majoribus Studiis,* and in the monastic discipline; sometimes he shows us an Englishman taking the road to Ireland seeking the double formation, intellectual and spiritual, *vel divinae lectionis vel continentioris vitae gratia illo secesserant;* to all who had embraced the monastic life, or were only seeking teaching in *lectio,* the Irish were welcoming in every way " offering them their daily food free, along with books and free instruction." Thus the Irish formation shed its radiance, not only in the isle of Erin where disciples of the first rank made a point of going to seek it, but further away, in England especially, since the relations between the two islands were of the easiest, and so far as the Continent as well. This is the praise which we have already read from the pen of Alcuin and we should not be surprised at a similar expansion by these same Irishmen, who had sought for a form of asceticism in " wandering for God ", so well indeed that one who is best versed in their history and in Celtic letters, Dom Louis Gougaud, has been able to write a whole book on *Irish Saints Outside Ireland.*

There have been lengthy discussions on the origins of this Irish culture, and some have gone so far as to ascribe its origins to

Byzantium, to the monks who were driven out by the Iconoclastic crisis—but they forget that this was never let loose till 754, and by that period the " learned men of Ireland " had won their reputation. The discussion has furthermore been placed more than once on the wrong track because people desired to make it bear principally, if not entirely, on the knowledge of classical letters, insisting on the study of Greek, of which the inhabitants of the island for a long time had only a vague smattering. M. M. Roger in his thesis of 1905 on *L'Enseignement des Lettres Classiques d'Ausone à Alcuin* (The Teaching of Classical Letters from Ausonius to Alcuin) went on to a judicious criticism of the views of M. Zimmer (*Pelagius in Ireland*, 1901), according to whom Ireland received the classical tradition, as well as the preaching of Christianity, from the Church of Great Britain from the fourth century onwards; this thesis should be viewed with certain definite reserves, but even taking these nuances into account, we can retain the essential, which for the period of the origins is more on the side of the preaching of the doctrine than the teaching of the liberal arts; there is nothing to show that St. Patrick set out to present himself as a man of letters and his mission was fruitful on another plane than that of the schools of the grammarians. Only, granting that Ireland never belonged to the Roman Empire, this preaching by a Church of Latin language, while not preventing the diffusion of the Celtic language and its local dialects, would suppose that with this there spread a knowledge of Latin; though we must not expect a people, even though very gifted, to yield of its own accord to a cultural tradition in a language not its own, we can count on the rare conscientiousness of the great Irish masters of the monastic life, a St. Finnian of Clonard, a St. Ciaran of Clonmacnois, a St. Fintan of Clonenagh, a St. Comgall of Bangor, a St. Brendan of Clonfert, a St. Columba of Iona, and rely on them that what they did for their disciples they would do well, including the study of the language which would be the vehicle of their instructions as of their prayers. We know that they profited by the lessons which they were able to receive from their first masters who came from Britain—and also from Gaul, for Gallican influences are perceptible, for example, in that very important liturgical monument known as the Antiphonary of Bangor—and their spiritual sons with them, though we could not as yet, in the sixth century, attribute to them important works by name.

St. Columba of Iona, according to his biographer St. Adamnan, spent much time in reading and writing; it was no doubt the Sacred Scriptures to which he applied himself in this way, and even if he is the author of the hymn *Altus prosator* which is often attributed to him, we cannot conclude from this that he devoted himself to a study of the liberal arts. One finds hellenisms there, which are indeed not foreign to the language of the Christian authors, and little known words, such as are often to be met with in the curious texts known as *Hisperica famina*: the very title of these sayings is an example of those non-classical derivatives of which the whole makes up a tangled vocabulary, in full conformity with the taste for complication, of which the less good of our island writers provide many an example; as for their origin, the adjective *hisperica* assigns them to the West, and to the ancients Ireland was, like Spain, the extreme Western end of the world; the more so as it is to Ireland, rather than to Spain or to Brittany, that we must probably attribute these compositions in a strange taste, of the VIth or at the most of the VIIth century; if, however, their influence was not so soon forgotten, it would be wrong to seek there for the dominant characteristic of the Irish genius, which we find capable of surpassing, and by a long way, this tangled rhetoric. Let us only retain, with the manifest exploitation of ecclesiastical Latin, the use of a fairly large number of Greek words: thus we once again find ourselves faced with the question of the relations between the first Irish writers and Hellenism; but it is not necessary to have a real knowledge of Greek in order to pilfer words from the glossaries, and it is not at this stage that we shall find the masters of the islands truly meriting the name of humanists; the influence will be needed of the lessons brought to the neighbouring Brittany, and thanks to her to Ireland by St. Theodore, who was from Tarsus and became Archbishop of Canterbury, and by his companion Abbot Hadrian. The merit of the Irish, who at this time had done excellently in the transmission of sacred letters as also in the teaching of monastic asceticism, would be to profit promptly by these precious exchanges. They had furthermore not waited for the arrival of Theodore in order to reap the teaching of the learned men of Greece, at least on a subject they had very much at heart, that of the computation, and it was from one of them that an Abbot of Bangor, Mosinu Mac Cumin, who died in 610, had learnt what he knew of the Paschal computation; this Mac Cumin, who is also called Sillan, and whom the manuscript of the Antiphonary of Bangor describes as a famous master, *famosus mundi magister*, had retained by heart this science of computation, which another monk of Bangor, Mocuoros Mac Cumin Semon, was to preserve by putting it into writing.

With the illustrious St. Columban, who having gone from Ireland into Gaul and then into Italy, was the founder of Luxeuil, then of Bobbio, we obtain the proof that the Irish schools, in the second half of the VIth century, could impart the teaching of the liberal arts, which is much more significant than the fact that the same Columban knew the Greek and Hebrew translation of his name of " dove ", for

such a small matter betokened neither a hebraic nor a hellenizing
strain. Through his biographer Jonas of Bobbio, who was so excellently informed, we know that Columban had studied grammar,
rhetoric, geometry, before he placed himself, for the study of the
Bible, at the school of the holy man Sinalus, then of St. Comgall
at Bangor; and to this knowledge his own writings bear witness, for
if his letters abound in quotations from the scriptures, a proof that
the texts were really familiar to him, he also allowed himself the
relaxation of writing Latin verses, hexameters and a poem made of
the little verses known as adonic, a simple dactyl followed by a
spondee or a trophee, and which in the classical poets one usually
finds joined to three sapphic verses to form a stanza of the same
name. Now, these metrical compositions of Columban, which pre-
suppose a certain knowledge of prosody, show us at the same time
that he had not only read verses of Virgil, but other ancient authors
such as Horace, Sallust, Ovid, of whom he slips memories into his
own verses, following a process of patchwork composition which
was to remain dear to the versifiers of the Middle Ages. It is Virgil,
here as elsewhere, who of all these classics is the most read, and other
Irishmen such as Adamnan, or Cellanus who died in 706 Abbot
of the " Scottish " monastery of Péronne, show likewise that they
had considerable recourse to him; but other ancient writers were to
follow him, read in their texts or more probably in extracts and
would contribute to the formation, in the domain of human letters,
of these Irish masters, whose teaching was so highly valued on the
subject of monastic spirituality.

People flocked from the Continent and from Brittany to study
the Sacred Scriptures in their school, in the knowledge of which
they had the reputation of being very advanced; when we read the
Ecclesiastical History of the English People, of the Venerable Bede,
so serene and objective, we are struck by seeing returning as a
leitmotif the ordered eulogy of the Irish wise men for being profoundly well versed in the biblical sciences, and this without a note
of jealousy which we find in another Englishman of the great class,
Aldhelm, when faced with this abundance in Ireland of studious
foreigners. It was thus that Bede was to write of the Frank Agilbert,
the future Bishop of Paris, that he had spent in Hibernia a fairly
long stay " in order to read the Scriptures there ", which would show
that he had spent as long in their study as could be done at the
time, and there are numerous prelates, priests, and princes of Christian
England of whom Bede writes the same thing, while of an Irishman
like St. Adamnan, the biographer of St. Columba, and the author of
a description of the Holy Land, founded on the account of his guest
Arculphe who had been there, he was to say that he was " instructed

in a very remarkable way ", *nobilissime instructus,* in the science of the Scriptures; we have seen that St. Columban had already given proof of his ability in this order, and these are not exceptions in the Ireland of that day. The Vulgate gradually became substituted for the ancient version used by St. Patrick, and which continued to be read after him, but the Irish manuscripts always preserved for a long time the traces of the earlier text; we can state this in particular as regards the psalter and the Epistles of St. Paul, and examples which served the Scots when they came onto the Continent preserve in a number of libraries the tradition of this Irish revision, which has retained the attention of historians of the biblical text and of its versions. We also have witnesses to the manner in which the masters of Erin, from the time before the Carolingian renaissance, commented on the sacred books; we no longer have the commentary on the Psalms which St. Columban had composed in his youth, according to Jonas of Bobbio; but there is a work of an Irishman of the VIIth century which owing to the name of its author found its way unduly among the writings of the great doctor of Hippo: it is a little treatise on the marvels of Sacred Scripture, *De Mirabilibus Scripturae Sanctae,* in which the author explains how the divine government works in the events which deviate from the ordinary course of nature, and which gives us some interesting details, not only on exegesis, but on the physique of the Irish; Aileran, who died in 664, has left us a *Mystical Interpretation* of the ancestors of Christ, that is to say of their names; but the more important works of Irish exegesis did not see the light till later, the commentary on Isaias by Joseph the Scot (died after 791) and above all, in the IXth century the works of Sedulius Scottus.

It is impossible not to give a high place to the activity of Irishmen in the domain of Canon Law. It does not sustain itself, as in other countries, from the official sources, the canons of councils or the decisions of pontifical authority: we hear of scarcely any synods meeting in Hibernia, and the celebrated collection *Hibernensis,* in sixty-seven books of which the classification scarcely seems to be ordered, is the work of canonists without official authority, a certain Ruben or Rubin Mac Conad, who died in 725, and Cuchuimne the wise, who was attached to the abbey of Iona and died about 745; their compilation thus goes back to the first quarter of the VIIth century. It is strongly sustained on Sacred Scripture, to the point of insisting on certain ordinances of the Old Testament which were no longer practised in the Christian Church, such as the jubilee year on the proscription of unclean animals; it is founded on the councils which were more or less correctly attributed to the age of St. Patrick and, naturally, on the great laws of general legislation, without forgetting the writings of the Fathers; the tendency of this compilation is clearly Roman and is opposed to the ancient and particular customs of the British and Celtic Churches as regards the tonsure or episcopal consecration, the appeal to Rome being the great recourse, whereas the role of the Bishops is relatively effaced. The diffusion of this canonical collection was considerable, even on the Continent, and they also used some Canones Adomnani of Irish origin. But another branch of canonical literature in which the influence of the Celtic islanders is dominant is that of the *Penitentials,* of which the most ancient is attributed to one of the St. Finnians of the VIth century, others having for their authors St. Columban, St. Cummean . . . ; from " tariffed " penances, in which sanctions were attached to each fault according to its gravity, the penitentials passed on to " satisfactory " penance, due to works of compensation or to commutations, which were called by the Irish name of *arrea,* and which contributed notably to the doctrine of indulgences. We know furthermore that the influence of St. Columban and the Columbanian monks counted for much in the diffusion of private penance in the West and in the practice of frequent confession.

The Irish conception of " wandering for God ", which led a number of ascetics to go into exile so that they might lead on the Continent austere and apostolic lives, led to the foundation in Gaul of regular Scottish monasteries, like the one which arose at Péronne when the relics of St. Fursy had been taken there (he died about the middle of the VIIth century) and which was known as *Perrona Scottorum;* the same was said of Fosses, the foundation to the head of which St. Gertrude of Nivelles had called St. Foillan, the brother of Fursy, that it was a *monasterium Scottorum,* and Einhard still refers to it as such. Several of these centres of Irish expansion had an important rôle to play when Charlemagne, having decided to invite foreign masters to France, Italians, Anglo-Saxons . . . in order to restore studies, included among them a certain number of Irish learned men. One of these was Clement, who became a professor at the Palatine school and remained there under Louis the Pious, before retiring to Wurzburg, whither he was attracted by the tomb of the great Irish missionary St. Kilian; another was perhaps Joseph the Scot, the commentator on Isaias, who addressed Latin poems to Charlemagne and to Alcuin; he was sent to Pavia, where later Lothair invited to the same position one of the numerous Dungals who made this thoroughly Irish name familiar to the people of the Continent. Another Dungal, who had written a curious letter to Charlemagne about the eclipse of 810, strange rather for the quality of its language than for the exactitude of its astronomical knowledge, and who finished his days, so it is believed, as a recluse at Saint-Denis, was attracted by Hildoard, Bishop of Cambrai, round whom had formed a whole circle of learned Scots in exile; by the researches of Traube we know of similar colonies at Rheims, where Dunchad taught, at Soissons, but especially at Laon, where stayed the famous John Scotus Eriugena, the friend of Bishop Hincmar, and where there taught after him learned men such as Hélie, the future Bishop of Angoulême, or Martin the Irishman; as for Sedulius, to whose name is usually joined the epithet of his origin, Scottus, it was at Liège that he settled, at the instigation of Bishop Hartgaire, who relied on his school of Saint-Lambert gaining by the knowledge of this master, capable, like the most learned of his compatriots, of applying himself with success to the most diverse disciplines.

If we have been able to discuss the extent of the Greek culture of the Irish " wise men " at the period of the origins—and we have seen that certain critics overestimated this—there is no doubt that several of the masters whom the Carolingian renaissance owed to Ireland were, as far as was possible in Western Europe, excellent hellenists; we must also add that they had largely increased their knowledge of Greek after their arrival in France, where they had access to the manuscripts of ancient authors which Ireland did not have at its disposal; but the zeal with which they profited from these increased resources is a title of honour for them, and they have contributed widely by their intelligent action to the renewal of contact with classical culture. The exegetists among them occupied themselves with copying the Greek text of the psalter, as we see in the case of Sedulius Scottus, the Evangelists or the Epistles of St. Paul, so as the better to understand books which they were thus able to study from nearer at hand than in Latin versions; they com-posed for their use bilingual glossaries, of which certain ones have been preserved for us, and translations of academic works, like those of the grammarian Priscieu, in which each Greek word was care-fully examined and interpreted. Several of them, at that period when Latin poetry was intensely cultivated, if not always worked at with a very individual accent, wished to compose in Greek similar exercises in versification, and better still than the laborious Sedulius Scottus, John Scotus Eriugena succeeded with real good fortune. He further-more applied his knowledge of Greek to more useful tasks, and he performed a work of no small importance in translating from Greek into Latin the writings attributed to St. Denys the Areopagite, of which we know the influence on medieval theology and spirituality; he performed the difficult task so well that Anastasius the Librarian wrote to Charles the Bald, of his astonishment and admiration at seeing how " a barbarian, living at the ends of the world ", could

attain to such an understanding of the classical languages that he
could translate texts of such profundity from one to the other.

The intellectual activity of this pleiad of learned Irishmen, in the
time of Charlemagne, of Louis the Pious, and Charles the Bald is
enough to justify an admiration such as that of Anastasius, even if
their work was not always well ordered, due to a lack of balance
which was no doubt caused by the period as much as by the men,
for it is not easy to create again a forgotten branch of knowledge and
to make it progress, applying it to the discussion of fresh problems,
without running the risk of proposing solutions which scarcely meet
the case. The ardour, however, with which these minds set to work
on something which they found highly congenial, never went to the
point of formal or intentional heresy; their errors do not arise from
a conscious intention to deviate from the pure doctrine, and the just
reproaches addressed then and since to a Scotus Eriugena, for such
a vigorous thought which however lacked the support of the firm
tradition of the schools, that in the following centuries was to sustain
the constructive efforts of the great doctors, have never gone to the
point of accusing him of this, even when he was compromised by
disciples who made an illicit use of his name. His great boldness in
attempting a philosophical and theological synthesis certainly suffered
from coming too soon, in a period when he was sustained above all
by pseudo-Denys, and in which he had not the means to bring to a
conclusion such a succession of ideas, but was recovering the thought
of older times by the Neo-Platonists whom he had first known in
the Latin sources.

The treatise *De divisione naturae*, which dates from 866, is in some
ways like the medieval " summas," but remains an isolated effort,
and could not, in spite of the rare intelligence of the thinker in
whom we may without exaggeration recognize genius, reach the aim
of his ambitious research. Numbers of his ideas are fertile, and
furthermore are joined up with a tradition; but it is not in the form
which he gives them that they will be able to make their mark. When
the great Irishman, to whom posterity has wished to give twice the
name of his island of origin by calling him Scotus Eriugena, strove to
give to his investigation of the divine and transcendent realities the
advantages of philosophic speculation, he adopted what was to be
the method of the best scholastic theology, but by doing so he drew
on himself the reproach of excessive rationalization. When, preoccupied as a good Platonist with the divine transcendence and the
return to God, he seems to go to the length of confusing created
beings with the eternal ideas like God Himself, he seems to be ahead
of the offence of pantheism or monism, but an attentive examination
of his thought will show that he is not really a pantheist, but there

are too many formulas in which he imprudently gives this impression. When, in order to combat the false idea of Gottschalk of a pre-destination equally compelling for good and for evil, which at the same time placed in peril human liberty and the divine will to save all men, he restores to divine sanctifying grace the whole reality of predestination, from which sin is excluded in that it is an absence, he pushes so far the idea of the universal return to God that it seems there is no longer a Hell, and the theologians who were to take their stand against this novelty were all the more severe to him in that the Irish doctors, who were great readers of Pelagius's commentary on the Epistles of St. Paul, were without sufficient reason said to be given to the Pelagian heresy. To Scotus Eriugena the famous lines could be applied :—

Let it be said : he dared too much, but his boldness was fine . . .
And since then lesser men have had better fortune.

But his influence, which was a regrettable one for some of the next generation and led them to the confines of heresy, had a useful effect on the really great thinkers of the School, or at least of a section of the School, who did not reject the whole of this premature effort. If the excesses of certain stragglers who appealed to Eriugena ended by attracting belated condemnations of his memory and his works, such as those of the Council of Paris in 1210 and of Honorius III in 1225, it is not in this heterodox use of his thought that we seek for the more exact picture of the Irish master. "The influence of Eriugena," concludes one of the last historians to make a fundamental study of him, M. Aimé Forest, "will continue to exercize itself through his translations and his commentaries on Denys, in an indirect fashion by important ideas already trans-mitted to the pre-scholastic writers. There is no doubt his ideas have been little understood in their profound sense; they however contribute under numerous aspects to form the capital of medieval thought."

Sedulius Scottus, whom we have seen settled at Saint-Lambert at Liège and whose biography we can follow anyway up to 858, is not a personality of the breadth of John Scotus, but he also merits our attention. To his Latin poems he wished to add some in Greek, but with less aptitude than Eriugena; like him he also commented on the grammarians, whose vogue at the time was a sign of the renais-sance of the liberal arts : his book *De Rectoribus Christianis,* or Mirror of Princes, written for Lothair II, contains chapters of prose in a framework of versified passages, in the fashion of the *Consolation* of Boethius; his *Collectaneum,* a collection of extracts from the Fathers and the classical writers, opens with a series of " proverbs of the Greeks ", and shows well the appetite for reading of these encyclopedic

men of learning; his commentary on the *Isagoge* of Porphyry is a
contribution to the study of the dialectic and the logic, also very much
in favour with his forerunners in the School. Sedulius is, however,
something different from a master of the liberal arts, and especially
of the *trivium;* he had applied the same method of the *collectaneum,*
in the method of the ancient exegetical catenas, for the explanation
of the Pauline Epistles, and also of St. Matthew, but this last work
had remained in manuscript; he had also commented on the letter
of St. Jerome to Pope Damasus on the subject of the scriptures.
Thus did he reply to the combined direction of the Carolingian
renaissance, which was to renew sacred studies even more than profane letters.

Other writers among those whom Sedulius himself calls " the wise
men come from Ireland ", *sophos Scottigenos,* rich in knowledge and
poor in money, have played diverse parts in this concert. An Irishman
who died as Bishop of Salzburg, Virgil (+784), had found in various
classical authors, Pliny, Macrobius, Martianus Capella, reasons for
believing in the existence at that time usually denied, of the anti-
podes, and this cosmology which was suspect for a long time, and
held the world to be a sphere, is to be found once again in John
Scotus. Guindmelus, who came to conduct a school in Ireland, was
a grammarian and a metrician; Dunchad, who taught at Saint-Rémi
at Rheims and wrote about dialectic, is above all a commentator of
the " astrology " of Martianus Capella, perhaps also, according to a
hypothesis of Traube, of the translation of Porphyry by Boethius (in
the manuscript he is described as " pontiff ", *pontificis Hibernensis);*
Clement Scot dedicates to Lothair a writing on grammar and his
works bring him near to the *Ars Malsachani,* " treatise of the verb ",
which M. Roger has edited and of which the author, Mac-Salchan, is
also an Irishman. There is also another, and we are assured of this
by the way in which he speaks of " notre Scottia ", " notre île
d'Hibernie " (our Scotia, our isle of Hibernia), the curious learned
man Dicuil, of whom we only know that he came to France in order
to teach, and that he was in relations with the court of Louis the
Pious, to whom he addressed verses constantly; a grammarian, following the fashion, and a commentator of Priscian, he treated grammati-
cal questions in verse, on which he had also prepared a literary
treatise; he is the author of a treatise in four books, with mingled
prose and verse, on the computation, but we specially owe to him a
geographical treatise, *Liber de mensura orbis terrae,* which he compiled in 825, according to former cosmographies, and in which he
gives us firsthand information about Ireland and the journeys of the
Irish monks. In a very different order of studies one of the numerous
Irishmen who bore the name of Dungal combated, in a work dedicated

to Louis the Pious and Lothair, *Liber contra Claudium*, the iconoclastic errors of Bishop Claudius of Turin, defending against him the cultus of the saints, of their images and their relics; in a poem which seems to belong to him he speaks of himself as " exiled from Ireland ", *Hibernicus exul;* he also wrote about astronomy.

We can then see how remarkable was the intellectual activity of the Irish in the early middle ages, and what a fertile contribution it brought to the renewal of Christian thought. The outbreak of the Scandinavian invasions in the IXth century unfortunately stopped the soaring flight of Ireland, and so seriously did the libraries suffer that when Brian Boru wished to restore studies to honour, he had to buy books from the Continent. But many of these treasures of the mind had been saved by the emigrants who, during the attacks of the Vikings, had found another cause for *peregrinatio.* We can find the echo of the eagerness with which Carolingian France had welcomed them, in a letter of Heiric of Auxerre, who himself owed much of his learning to the Irish of the colony of Laon: " Here we have almost the whole of Ireland, despising the sea and its dangers, transporting itself to our shores with a company of its philosophers; the more a Scot is well instructed and able, the more readily does he decide on this exile, knowing it to respond to the wishes of a new Solomon." Dom Gougaud, who quotes his text (about 866) is right in noting an oratorical accent which tends to be a little forced; but he is no less right in stressing that such testimonies allow us to appreciate " in what esteem foreigners held Irish learning at its finest moment ".

Saint Malachy Seen By Saint Bernard
By ALEXANDRE MASSERON

IN the literary work of St. Bernard, which is so abundant and so varied, and which extends to all the domains of religious knowledge and to all the ecclesiastical affairs of his age, there is only one biography: that of one of his contemporaries, of a prelate of "the end of the earth", whom he had only met three times and for a very short time, at periods of his life when he was at the height of his fame, and when the gravest and most anxious controversies of Christianity were constantly dragging him from his cloister to travel, as peacemaker and reformer, all the roads of Europe.

Such a strange choice of a person of whom most of the Frenchmen of the XIIth century, even if they were clerics, had never heard, leaves us at first rather astonished. When, however, we have come to know the motives, we shall perhaps think that it is the purest earthly glory of Malachy O'Morgair, the Archbishop of Armagh, to have won, in a few days and as if by assault, the friendship and the veneration of St. Bernard, who, if he lacked the power to canonize him, has nevertheless presented him to the world as a saint, and, on the anniversary of his death, implored his intercession before the monks of Clairvaux: "O dazzling torch, light shining in the darkness who, with the radiance of your miracles and your merits, illumine our prison and spread joy in our city, drive from our hearts the darkness of vice by the brilliance of your virtues! Star of the morning, all the more sparkling because you are the neighbour of the day and more like the sun, deign to go before us so that we also may walk in the brightness, as the sons of light and not as the sons of darkness! Dawn which was seen to break forth on the earth, daylight whose fires illuminate the sublime regions of the sky, grant to us to participate in that light which you diffuse in the distance and of which you now experience the delight, by the grace of Our Lord Jesus Christ Who being God reigns with the Father and the Holy Ghost for ever and ever. Amen."

:-:   :-:   :-:

In the presence of these unexpected honours rendered by St. Bernard to Malachy, of this ardent devotion, do we not feel some embarrassment, and even some shame, if we own that the notoriety of the Archbishop of Armagh has another source, and this a troubled one, without which we might even be unaware of his existence ? As it is not impossible that a text of St. Bernard has been skilfully or cynically exploited in this venture, we must make a brief allusion to it.

Prophecy of the Popes . . . Prophecy of St. Malachy . . . the two expressions have become synonymous! At every pontifical election, this all too famous document, of which everyone has heard more or less, is loudly exhumed by the augurs who wish to force the secret of the future; the Archbishop of Armagh periodically enjoys an ephemeral popularity, of which his holy memory, more discreetly maintained by the Abbot of Clairvaux, had no need.

We know that it is a matter of one hundred and eleven devices which point out fairly clearly up to the time of Urban VII, then with enigmas of learned obscurity, the Popes of the future until the Last Judgment . . . from which we are only separated by six Popes after Pius XII !

Why was St. Malachy chosen to endorse the responsibility of this strange swindle of the end of the XVIth century ? We can at least suspect the reason why. The first device is concerned with Celestine II, who came to the See of St. Peter in 1143; now it was in the reign of his predecessor, Innocent II, that St. Malachy in 1139 made the journey to Rome where we are given to understand that the Prophecy of the Popes would have been composed. On the other hand, the attribution of this sibylline text, fabricated in Italy, to a person from a distant country and one difficult of access, was of a nature to deepen the mystery and to put too curious seekers off the track. Finally, had not St. Bernard written: " Neither the gift of prophecy, nor that of revelations were lacking to Malachy ", in reporting, but on the faith of another, a certain number of marvellous facts? What more was needed, as long as one was not lacking in audacity, to try and make these strange pontifical devices pass with the authority of the Archbishop of Armagh, although the absolute silence of St. Bernard on the subject remained an argument which was not easy to refute ?

Nor was the swindle an isolated one! There was specially circulated, in the name of St. Malachy, a prophecy about the Church in Ireland, which was to flourish again after seven centuries of oppression. It was Mabillon himself who discovered it in the archives of the Abbey of Einsiedeln, and he wrote on the subject: " The document was clearly composed for St. Bernard, even at the period when the latter was working on his Life of Saint Malachy . . . Clairvaux, the fact is certain, preserved the memory of many of the prophecies of St. Malachy, and of this one in particular." But the letter of the would-be Mabillon is also a forgery, as has been demonstrated by Father Grosjean, S.J., of the Society of the Bollandists. Its authenticity is

no better than that of the Prophecy of the Popes but its fortune has
luckily been less tumultuous!

The Archbishop of Armagh had nothing to do with this spurious
celebrity.

:-:   :-:   :-:

The Irish had read the works of St. Bernard; they had admired
them; they knew how immense was their diffusion and that the
brilliance and originality of the style were not inferior to the elevation
of the thought or the conquering ardour of the faith. They thought
that nobody was better able than the Abbot of Clairvaux to make live
again the fine and holy figure of him for whom they wept, to preserve
it piously and faithfully for the memory of men, and to ensure his
radiance beyond the too narrow limits of the country where Malachy
had waged his rough and heroic combat. Their request was presented
by Congan, the Cistercian Abbot of Inisnoulagh, which was indirectly
a foundation of Clairvaux, a grand-daughter of Mellifont, which issued
from Monasternenagh.

"Bernard," says Georges Goyau, "threw himself on his pen to
glorify this lamp, who late in the evening had bathed with a calming
light the dark and mysterious anguish which might still remain in
his soul." His eagerness is not a conjecture of French literature; we
have the proof in the Preface of the *Life*, addressed to Abbot Congan;
it is not only to his appeal that Bernard is going to respond, but to
the appeal of the whole Church in Ireland, which is a Church of
saints; he lets the enthusiasm break out of which his soul is full;
he wishes "to give back to the world him of whom the world was
not worthy"; he wishes to celebrate this truly holy man, this model
of wisdom, this model of virtue, who placed him in the rank of his
dearest friends and from whom he received, on his death-bed, the
last blessing: "It is with a most ready heart," he concludes, "that
I obey, especially as it is not a page of eloquence which you seek
from me, but an account. I will do all I can to make this account
simple and clear, capable of instructing pious men without crushing
the delicate ones. As to its truth, I am sure of that, for it is from
you that I have received these elements, and you have no doubt only
reported to me that of which you had complete certitude."

Dom L. Gougaud wrote in 1911 in *Les Chrétientés Celtiques*:
"Thanks to St. Bernard, his biographer and friend, no figure, no life
of those times is so well known as those of Malachy". But the fresh
discoveries of the religious history of Ireland in the twelfth century
have not confirmed these rather too optimistic views. Also Father
Grosjean has recently expressed a rather disturbing scepticism: "The

work of St. Malachy only appears to us in the distorting mirror of his panegyric by St. Bernard, which is more eloquent than worthy of belief without reserve." And again: " The eulogy of the hero is made at the expense of the good reputation of his compatriots, as if to the detriment of truth ".

The authority and the competence of the learned Bollandist, who has twice returned to the question, and more or less in the same terms, do not allow us to call in question that the mirror is distorting, though future exhumations may modify the perspective. But it is permissible to inquire at what angles the mirror has specially shown itself unfaithful and who must bear the responsibility.

What was the value of the documents sent from Ireland to Clairvaux, and to what extent was the picture which they gave of the abuses, not to say the state of anarchy, which St. Malachy had to fight, a faithful one ? To what extent also did the monks allow themselves to be drawn on, more or less consciously, to accumulate dark colours " to the detriment of truth ", to make the opposition more violent and the glory of their Archbishop more brilliant, in extolling his merits.

No doubt we shall never know precisely, because these documents are lost. Besides, St. Bernard neither had the time nor the means for controlling them. It would be rash to accuse him of falsifying them. But it is possible that he interpreted them as a panegyrist rather than as a historian, and without ever forgetting that the life of a saint should be written to serve " as a mirror and an example and in a sense as a condiment to the lives of those who are on earth ". One would perhaps be inclined to reproach him for having, here and there, a little too much abused the figures of rhetoric, and sacrificed too much to an excessive love of contrasts.

Should not all this, however, remain in the background if, from the Ireland which St. Bernard only knew most imperfectly and by hearsay, we pass to the Irishman with whom he had lived familiarly and whose gentle and calming influence he had experienced, in hours heavy with anguish when he felt himself crushed by the misfortunes of the Church, " feeble in heart and broken in body ", as he himself wrote of it ?

Here we have personal memoirs which St. Bernard will be able to use to give us a portrait of Malachy, personal memories which had remained singularly precise, the memory especially of conversations at Clairvaux, the memory of the direct impression, which was received from the first contact, that the foreigner was a saint, a man isolated, privileged by grace, in a world gone astray in which there were scarcely any prelates who were saints.

Information coming from outside only confirmed Bernard in a

certitude which he had acquired on his own; if this was indispensable for him in order to write a biography properly so-called, he could draw from another source to show us, in the person of St. Malachy, the ideal type of Bishop who, by the heroic practice of all the Christian virtues, and particularly of poverty, humility and charity, accomplished in Ireland a work of reform and pacification analogous to that to which he had consecrated his life.

St. Bernard was a master of moral dissection; nobody knew better than he did how to pass beyond external appearances, which were often deceptive, so as to reach the inmost recesses of the human soul. He was a rigorous observer, and in his treatise *Degrees of humility and of pride* he has traced for us silhouettes of monks suffering from curiosity, thoughtlessness, vain joy, boasting, eccentricity, arrogance, presumption, etc. and who in less experienced eyes would have passed for holy people; he has however not been deceived and has had no difficulty in unmasking these more or less conscious impostors. Nor did he make any mistake from the time of his first meeting with the Archbishop of Armagh; it was a saint who was arriving at Clairvaux from the "ends of the earth" endowed with all the graces and all the blessings of Heaven, whom Providence had raised up at a time when sanctity was rare and in which St. Bernard heard the menace of these words of Christ: "The charity of most men will grow cold, as they see wickedness abound everywhere". Perhaps, however, he did not suspect that a few years later he would throw himself in the arms of this foreigner?

:-:   :-:   :-:

In 1139, St. Malachy had formed the plan to go to Rome, to inform the Pope of the religious affairs of his country, and specially to obtain confirmation for the erection of the See of Cashel as the second metropolitan See, and that the Archbishops of Armagh and Cashel should receive the pallium. He fulfilled this plan in spite of lively opposition from the monks and the people, who feared that his long absence would have fatal consequences and were afraid that he might die on the way. He was received with extreme good-will by Innocent II, who appointed him as legate for the whole of Ireland, in the place of Gilbert, Bishop of Limerick, whose age and infirmities prevented him for the future from carrying out the functions.

However, the first favour for which Malachy implored the Pope was something quite different, and that he begged, St. Bernard tells us, "with many tears", that he might retire to Clairvaux to live there until his death. This was now his chief desire, though he had not forgotten that the original aim of his long and difficult journey was something quite different. Innocent II refused; he judged that Malachy's holy activity was indispensable for the Church in Ireland, of which the Archbishop of Armagh knew better than anyone else the needs and the unusual situation.

What had happened and what was the cause of this change in the Irishman's plans?

Attracted by Bernard's reputation for sanctity, whose name was on all lips, St. Malachy had wanted to know this wonderful man, who had made the reform of the Order of St. Benedict to triumph, who struggled without respite against abuses and scandals, and who had re-established the unity of the Church, in the lamentable affair of the schism of Anacletus II, when he had specially brought the King of England back to the party of Innocent II. The Archbishop, on his way to Italy, had made a détour so as to visit Clairvaux, and there he had felt all the aspirations of his youth take on a new vigour in his heart. Was it not in placing himself at school to a recluse and in leading under his direction a life of austerity, to the stupefaction and even to the dismay of many of his compatriots, that he had begun to snatch himself from the world? Had he not raised the Abbey of Bangor from its ruins and founded that of Iseragh? And was it not in spite of himself and almost compelled by force that he had abandoned solitude and accepted the burdens of the episcopate? " He saw my brethren," wrote St. Bernard, " and he was touched with compunction, and he edified them greatly by his presence and by his words." Clairvaux seemed to him the port of salvation where he could finally cast his anchor and which would assure for him until his death a foretaste of eternal joys.

" It was granted to me to see this man," adds St. Bernard; " I enjoyed the sight of him and his conversation, which gave me new strength, and, sinner as I am, I found grace in his eyes." Humility halted the impulse of his pen; it is not difficult to supplement his silence; the master had, even more than his subjects, inspired the decision of the Archbishop.

On his return from Rome, where he stayed about a month, Malachy passed back by Clairvaux, and " sighing deeply ", he confided his sorrow to St. Bernard: the Pope was sending him back to Ireland and was opposed to the realization of his dearest desire. But the lessons which he could not receive himself, he wished should be received by some of his compatriots. He chose four whom he left with his saintly friend, saying to him: " I beg you to keep them instead of me, so that they may learn from you what they will then teach to us."

Some time later, when he had returned to his island, Malachy sent other Irishmen to Clairvaux, so that they could also become Cistercians. They bore a letter and a crosier. St. Bernard experienced a great joy. " The letter shows that you love me; my enfeebled body

will lean on that crosier; these brothers serve God in a spirit of
humility"; giving the Archbishop some advice in regard to the erection
of the future Abbey; he added: " May the name of the Lord be
blessed in all ages, for having brought to birth sons whom I have
in common with you; they are flowers whom your preaching has
planted, that my exhortations have watered, and which God has
caused to blossom."

We have preserved for us two other letters, addressed by St. Bernard
to St. Malachy. One of them is only a short note, in which the
Abbot of Clairvaux complains that he has only been able to send to
Ireland " but little seed ", that is to say religious who were not yet
sufficiently instructed, not sufficiently advanced in the ways of perfection. But in the second he gives free flow to the effusions of his
heart: " How much sweetness your words have for me, O my father,
and what joy I have in remembering your Holiness! Everything that
there can be in my soul of tenderness or religious respect, my love
for your Charity takes possession of it altogether. Many words are
not needed, where the sentiments are very lively. I am confident that
the spirit of God which lives in you, will assure you that the little
which I am belongs to you completely. Do not forget, my well
beloved father, the soul of a poor man who is united with you by
the bonds of charity; deign to remember the soul of your poor man.
I do not wish to commend myself to you once again, since I have so
long been glorifying myself in the Lord, that my unworthiness has
found grace in the eyes of your Holiness, but I pray that this friendship, which is not new, may became greater every day."

Then, with a tranquil audacity, which would only astonish those
who were unaware of the tone with which this simple monk used
to lecture Popes and Kings, and all powerful people whether they
were Churchmen or not, St. Bernard gives advice to the Archbishop.
It is vibrant with his solicitude, not to say anxiety, for his sons who
were so far from him; he had only allowed them to leave for Ireland,
because it would have seemed criminal to him to give a refusal to
Malachy's prayers; he implores him on no pretext to weaken his
vigilance or his care. This Abbey of Mellifont is a new establishment,
which requires that all the more zeal should be consecrated to its
foundation in that the country has not had the experience of monastic
discipline: " We implore you in the name of the Lord not to with-
draw your hand, and to complete happily what you have begun so
well." One can the better understand the anxiety of St. Bernard
in that some French Cistercians had returned from Ireland discouraged perhaps by customs with which they were scarcely familiar.

The Archbishop, a true disciple of the Master of humility, accepted
these admonitions with gratitude; and we are assured that his friend-

ship for the Abbot of Clairvaux was even increased; for, if we are
badly informed on the relations which he could have had with him
from 1142 to 1148, this gap is filled up by the account of his last
visit to the abbey, of which he had experienced the holy and powerful
fascination, and where he had the consolation to come to die; it is
the most moving page of the book written by St. Bernard at the
request of Abbot Congan.

The question of the pallium had not been settled following on the
first journey of St. Malachy to Rome in 1139. The Pope had refused
to grant this privilege to the Archbishops of Ireland until a council
had asked him for it. For reasons of which we know little, this
council did not meet until 1148, at Inispatrick, and fifty Bishops
there decided to take fresh steps with Eugenius III, who was at that
time in France, to remind him of the promises of Innocent II. St.
Malachy, the Papal Legate, was naturally charged with this. But,
after visiting Scotland and England, he was prevented for political
reasons from going immediately to France. When he arrived,
Eugenius III had returned to Italy; St. Bernard was inclined to see
in this delay a providential interposition, which allowed the Archbishop to pay a final visit to the abbey where he had always desired
to die. "With what resplendent brilliance did not the rays of that sun
make our Clairvaux shine! What cheerfulness there was on that feast
day which the Lord has granted us and on which he arrived among
us! What transports of joy! Sick, and with uncertain steps, I rushed
along directly and threw myself in his arms; it is a grace which is
granted us from Heaven . . ." And all the monks joined with their
Abbot, to celebrate the goodness, the affability, even the gaiety of
their guest. These were days of happiness, but were to be singularly
brief: from the 13th or 14th of October till the 18th, the feast of
the evangelist St. Luke, when Malachy, having said the conventual
Mass with great piety, was seized by an attack of fever and had to
take to his bed: "We were all sick with him," writes St. Bernard.
Sadness succeeded to joy, but they persuaded themselves, they wished
to persuade themselves that it was a mild crisis and that no danger
was threatening him. The religious paid marked attention to him:
for each one it was delightful to see him, and even more delightful
to tend him. He accepted all the remedies which were offered him,
but out of charity. He knew that his hour was near: God Who in
His mercy had led him to Clairvaux, would not refuse it to him to
die there. "My miserable body will find its rest here; as for my
soul, God will provide for it, He Who saves those who place their
hope in Him." He asked for Extreme Unction and the Viaticum, and
as all the monks wished to go up to his cell, he opposed this, and he
would go down to them. And yet "he said that death was at the

door. Who would have thought that this was a dying man ? He alone and God could know. His face was no paler nor thinner, there were no wrinkles in his forehead; no veil over the eyes; the nostrils were not pinched; the lips were not tightly pressed; the teeth remained white, the neck full, the shoulders straight; there was no sign of exhaustion . . ."

Appearances were deceptive. The illness rapidly became worse. On All Saints' Day the whole community were collected around his bedside: " We sang as we wept, we wept as we sang . . ." But if his declining forces prevented St. Malachy from uniting himself with the voices of his brethren, he and he alone did not weep, he and he alone was festive: " At twilight, he was not approaching the twilight, but the dawn." The fever became more intense; his body was covered with perspiration. He said to those who were assisting him: " I have desired with a great desire to eat this Pasch with you. I give thanks to the supreme Mercy, for I shall not be disappointed." And he consoled them by his gentle words: " Remember me; if it is allowed me, I shall not forget you. And it will be allowed me. I believe in the goodness of God, and everything is possible for him who believes. I have loved God, I have loved you, and charity always triumphs." He then raised his eyes to Heaven and blessed them, placing his hands on them: " My God, keep them in Your grace and with them all those whom my words and my ministry have caused to consecrate themselves to Your service." And, as his hour had not yet come, he told them to go and take a little rest. The religious returned to his bed about the middle of the night; to the singing of hymns, psalms and spiritual cancticles, Malachy, Bishop and Legate of the Holy Apostolic See, fell asleep happily in the Lord, as if he had been, by their hands, carried to Heaven by angels. And it was really as if he had fallen asleep; all eyes were fixed on him and nobody could say at what moment his soul had left the earth; his face had preserved the same expression of life, the same serenity that he showed in sleep. " He had not changed, but he had changed us all; tears and lamentations stopped suddenly; sadness became joy, and the lamentations gave way to songs of triumph."

Reason forbade St. Bernard to weep over this happy end which was " the gate of life ". He at least tried to persuade himself: " Malachy, our friend, has fallen asleep and should I be in tears? This would be in conformity with our human habits, but it would be unreasonable . . . he has been taken into the joy of the Lord and should I give myself up to sorrow ?" Did St. Bernard obey cold reason ? We have the right to doubt this, we do indeed doubt it, when we remember how much of human tenderness from the depths of his heart he managed to conceal and how he had to own himself conquered after the death of his brother Gerard. He had officiated apparently impassive at the funeral ceremony, then he had resumed before his religious his commentaries on the Song of Songs. When he reached this verse, " Black are the tents they have in Cedar; black are Solomon's own curtains ", he had to stop suddenly, incapable of dissembling any longer: "I own, I am conquered; it is necessary for me to reveal all that I suffer . . ." Meditation on the secred book had transformed itself into a heart-rending lamentation, in which St. Bernard sought an excuse for his tears in the tears which Jesus had shed before the sepulchre of Lazarus, and in which he asked no more from God than to set an end and a limit to his sorrow.

It was the same with him when his saintly friend fell asleep in his arms, and he could only follow the advice which he gave to the religious of Ireland, when he announced to them the death of their father: "Nobody would be astonished if affection drew out lamentations, if desolation made the tears to flow; we must only moderate their course. . ." But it is on other sentiments that he insists in this letter, as in the two sermons which he preached at Clairvaux on the anniversary of the " passage to the heavenly country" of St. Malachy: " From heaven, my beloved, there descends to you today an abundant benediction ". Sorrow must give place to joy, to joy of having such a powerful protector near to God, whose prayers will be more effective and whose ever active charity will have increased; in the order of things invisible, which are eternal, Malachy is ever alive, Malachy is blessed. On earth he was a great model of perfection. It was by his example and by his words that the religious of Ireland must guide themselves so that each day they might make new progress; it was in his footsteps and in the soft perfume of his virtues that the Cistercians of Clairvaux must " run ". Never did St. Bernard exalt with so much authority, assurance and certainty the merits and virtues of a man whom the Church had already placed on her altars.

:-:   :-:   :-:

The Archbishop had arrived for the first time at Clairvaux with a wretched turn-out. He himself rode a horse of poor quality which had been given him at York by a nobleman, who later entered the Order of Citeaux, and who excused himself that he only had this beast of burden to offer to the religious of whom several had to go on foot: " Saddle him for me," Malachy had replied; " it is all that I need and will do for a long time." In this poor cortège there were to be seen no mounts bearing precious stones, with harness plated with gold and silver; nor were any of those sumptuous clothes to be seen, which resembled the dress of women.

Everything was simple, everything was almost poverty-stricken.

nothing in his clothes distinguished Malachy from his companions.
What a powerful introduction was this very destitution to the austere
monk who, in the treatise *De officio et moribus episcorum*, had
lashed the luxury of the prelates with his sarcasms.

Later, St. Bernard learnt from the Irishmen that Malachy had no
servants, no lay-clerks, no farms, no villas, no revenues of any sort,
nothing belonging to himself, not even a house! He was constantly
on the roads, always travelling on foot, going through the parishes
to preach the Gospel, and if he absolutely had to take some rest,
stopping in those religious houses which he had founded all over
Ireland, where he would sit at the common table. When he had been
called to the succession by the dying Archbishop of Armagh, and
when the Bishop of Lismore and the Papal Legate, Gilbert of
Limerick, pressed him to accept this charge, he started by obstinately
refusing, alleging that he had " a spouse, from whom he was not
permitted to separate himself ". Being at last compelled to accept,
he only did so on the condition that he should be allowed, if peace
was restored to the Church, to " return to his first spouse and friend,
poverty, from which he was being dragged ". Concord being re-
established after about five years of continual struggles, during which
he had braved death and escaped the worst ambushes, he resigned
his charge; as his former See of Connor was occupied, he divided it
into two parts, only keeping for himself the smaller: " Where are
then," wrote St. Bernard, " those churchmen haggling over questions
of boundaries, and whom the possession of a straggling village incites
to perpetual hatred? Are there any men to whom these words of the
prophet are more applicable than to them: ' that so coveted Galaad's
lands, every mother's womb he would rip open ' ". (Amos, I, 14).

Poverty, humility, disinterestedness, virtues of the apostolic times,
virtues despised today, were they only to be seen flowering once more
in this foreigner? We should be tempted to suspect this astonishing
portrait which St. Bernard has made of his friend, clearly allowing
himself to be led along by his satirical spirit and his polemical
temperament, for he seems to contrast with the Archbishop of
Armagh all the other Bishops of Christendom, who like him are the
heirs of the Apostles, and who share their heritage with him, but in
a very strange form: " These establish their dominion over the
clergy; Malachy, who has complete liberty, makes himself the servant
of all. These eat without evangelizing, or evangelize in order to eat;
Malachy, imitating St. Paul, eats in order to evangelize. These judge
that piety is for profit and display; Malachy only claims for his part
of the heritage work and burdens. These think they are happy if
they have extended their domains; Malachy's glory is to hear of
charity. These heap up in their granaries and collect in their casks

what will furnish their tables; he assembles in the deserted places
and the solitudes men with whom he will people Heaven. These,
though they receive pennies, first-fruits, oblations, and by the favour
of Caesar market-dues, tributes and other revenues *ad infinitum*, do
not ask for less if they have enough to eat and drink; Malachy, who
possesses nothing of all that, nevertheless enriches many with the
abundance of his faith. These place no limit to their cupidity and
their solicitude; Malachy, who desires nothing, does not even think
of the morrow. These exact from the poor what they give to the rich;
as for him, he asks from the rich for what is necessary to feed the
poor. These empty the purses of their subordinates; he in order to
obtain the remission of their sins, loads the altars with vows and
peace-making offerings. These raise up to the sky magnificent palaces,
with towers and walls; Malachy, who has nowhere to rest his head,
continues his work of an evangelist. These travel on horseback,
escorted by a crowd of people who live at their expense; Malachy,
surrounded by pious brethren, goes on foot, carrying the bread of
angels, to satiate famished souls. These do not know the men of the
people; he instructs them. These honour the powerful and the tyrants;
he punishes them. A truly apostolic man, whom so many and such
great miracles have made famous!"

A portrait drawn in violent contrasts, and in which the vices of
" those "—what disdain in the pronoun *illi*, repeated twenty times!—
are only harshly branded in order to glorify St. Malachy. In the
preface to the *Life*, had not St. Bernard already said to Abbot Congan,
that if one only raised one's eyes to the " columns of the Church
themselves " one only saw " smoky wicks " among those whose rôle
was to enlighten the nations ? Had this Irishman alone been an
exception to the general law of a period which suffered from a scarcity
of men, and in which it was enough not to be too bad to appear
excellent?

Besides, miracles of all sorts broke out at his feet, miracles which
his compatriots had gathered together with pious solicitude, and
of which they had sent the account to St. Bernard, so that he should
include them in the *Life*. And each of these miracles, of which the
circumstances of the time and place are almost always stated precisely,
is for the Abbot of Clairvaux the occasion to throw some light upon,
not only the power of the wonder-worker, but also the diverse aspects
of his friend's admirable sanctity. Among these aspects, here is one
that we have scarcely had the occasion of meeting with up to now.
Malachy received one day the visit of a man who feared God, and
occupied an honourable position in the world, and who came to
complain to him that his soul was sterile: he begged the saint to
obtain for him the gift of tears. At such a request, which was so

unexpected on the part of a layman, Malachy could not repress a smile, and touching with his mouth the mouth of his visitor, he said to him: " Let it be as you ask ". The tears flowed immediately.

Let us retain the smile of the Archbishop of Armagh in this curious miracle. This smile St. Bernard knew well for he had often seen it straying on the lips of his friend, who, in his work as an apostle of the Gospel and a reformer, had brought a gentleness and a serenity which he had not always been able to preserve himself. Malachy had a great power of attraction which nobody had been able to escape, but which the Abbot of Clairvaux experienced more than any other, and to which he constantly returned: Malachy edified those who surrounded him by his behaviour, by his exterior aspect, by his modest ways, by the expression of his face which had about it nothing austere and the gravity of which was tempered by playfulness. His self-denial and his zeal were at the service of all; and even to the wicked he showed his gentleness. He no doubt had sometimes to show himself severe and to be angry, but " he had his anger in hand; if it was called for, it showed itself, but it never escaped from his control; it obeyed him, he was never carried away by it; it did not burn him, he made use of it . . . if you had seen him plunged into the tumult of affairs and overwhelmed with cares, you would have thought that he was only born for his country; if you had seen him alone, living on his own, you would have thought he only lived in God and for Him."

" Malachy," comments George Goyau, " had reconciled the severe Bernard with a certain way of laughing, at least of smiling . . . and it seemed that his example had resolved the problem which all his life had crucified the Abbot of Clairvaux," the problem of a religious whom the imperious necessities of action have dragged in spite of himself from the contemplative life and from the divine joys of his cell.

When he left Clairvaux in 1139 to visit Rome and Innocent II, the Archbishop of Armagh thought he had found the true road along which he would travel till his death: to take the white cowl of Citeaux and to place himself, he who had been primate of Ireland, at the school of a simple monk, to become a saint under his direction. When he was forced to return to Ireland he endeavoured, when founding Cistercian abbeys, to make his compatriots follow the teaching which he had received. He no doubt thought, in his humility, that he had never been more than a disciple, though he had really brought a lesson to Clairvaux, a lesson to which St. Bernard assured an immense acclaim, in spite of the historical errors which the learned have been able to refer to in his work: Malachy performed many miracles, but " the first and the greatest " was himself.

Irish Art and its Influence on the Continent

By FRANCOISE HENRY
Of University College, Dublin

ONE of the most interesting aspects of the history of Ireland during the early Middle Ages, is that very special art which developed in the Irish monasteries and which Irish monks carried to the Continent where it has been, over and over again in different circles, the object of a strong admiration and the starting-point for imitations of every kind.

Her history even predisposed Christian Ireland towards an art of singular originality. The heir of ancient and essentially abstract traditions, she preserved them in all their intensity, scarcely touched by any reflection of Roman ways. Other elements—oriental and barbaric—came to incorporate themselves in this primitive root, but without profoundly modifying the inner logic. And an experience of the century prepared this technical virtuosity which gave a surprising acuteness to this art of which the only means of expression was for centuries perpetually renewed combinations of lines and colours.

According to a tradition which goes fairly far back, Patrick brought with him artisans—masons, gold and silversmiths and founders in bronze—and it goes without saying that he brought with him books, copies of the Gospels certainly, and probably psalters. Masons or stone-cutters, whether they came from Gaul or from Great Britain, no doubt had the custom of tracing in the stone those crosses or those monograms inscribed in circles which rise above funereal inscriptions or are stamped on the lintels of the doors of churches at the end of the Roman times. They found themselves faced with local sculptors who had the custom of covering the surface of stones which had scarcely been roughed out with a network of curved lines tangled irregularly and of carving massive statues in which the human form was scarcely conjured up. The fusion between the two methods did not take long to produce itself. The workers in metal no doubt did not have much to learn from those talented artists such as were the Irish gold and silversmiths and enamellers, except perhaps a fresh care for symmetry in decoration and some forms of objects not in use. Books represented the great novelty in that country where all instruction had been oral and where the only known form of writing was oghamic, a sort of figure, unusable for anything except a short sentence. The manuscripts brought by St. Patrick were no doubt but little decorated, but there were probably found in them, as in several manuscripts of the end of the empire, enlarged and lightly ornamented capitals at the beginning of the most important paragraphs.

These were the first bases. But there would soon be added, above all in the decoration of manuscripts, elements due to the close relations which existed between the monasteries of Egypt and Syria and those of Ireland[1]. It is to this oriental influence that we must attribute the popularity of interlaced ornaments and that of red stippling employed whether in seed-plots or in circles round a decorative theme or a letter, and the custom of introducing into the manuscript pages full of ornaments (carpet-pages). Other motifs, and especially the animal amid interlacing ornament, appeared later following on contacts with the Irish and the Saxons.

The period of semi-seclusion, when Ireland found herself more or less isolated from the rest of the Christian world by the barrier of England which had once again become pagan, a period which reaches from the arrival of the Saxons (middle of the Vth century) till their conversion (first half of the VIIth century) sees the first manifestations, at first rather timid, of this art. They are worn ornamented monoliths, even with an irregular surface, of a carved or sculptured cross in light relief (Pl. 1, 1A.), sometimes accompanied with a decoration made of some curved or angular lines; there are objects of bronze, pins, basins, etc., which have a curvilinear decoration, whether executed in very light relief, or heightened with a base of red enamel.

A manuscript which goes back to the end of the VIth century, the Cathach, is also all soberly ornamented: one only finds in it capitals which come unravelled, or swell out in curves, underlined with a vivid yellow and accompanied with a circle of red stippling. Similar manuscripts were clearly taken by the missionaries who left Ireland at the end of the VIth and the beginning of the VIIth century, and among others by St. Columban and his companions. And in the monasteries which they founded on the Continent, Luxeuil, Saint-Gall, Bobbio, the missionary monks and their pupils decorated others. From that remote date, Irish art which was still in the lisping stage, began that swarming across Europe which was to continue for centuries. We have from the monastery of Bobbio some manuscripts which go back to the first years of the monastery—one of them belongs to the time when Atalanus, the immediate successor of

---

[1] These relations, which have often been stressed, among others by Dom Gougaud, Kingsley Porter, etc., are not only indicated by archæological signs, but also by texts of which the most striking is perhaps the passage of a poem contained in the *Antiphonary of Bangor* (Ambrosian, MS., c. 5, second half of the Vth century) or the rule of the monastery of Bangor in the North of Ireland and described as *vinea vera ex Aegypto transducta*.

Columban, was Abbot, about 620. They are written in a form of script which at that time was characteristic of Irish manuscripts, or else in the form of writing which participates at the same time in that used in the other monasteries of Italy and in Irish characters. Manuscripts with ornamented letters were brought from Ireland, such as the *Antiphonary of Bangor* (Pl. 1, 1B.) And they aredecorated with ornaments similar to those used at the same period in Ireland; as on pillars of stone spirals burst out, like branches, and from the point of a letter, red stippling covers the down stroke of the capitals; in a manuscript there appears a carpet-page. In the other Irish foundations of the same period, we have less evidence of this " insularity " of the Irish monasteries of the Continent, but the Church of Saint-Gall still preserves one of the little bells which sculptors show us in the hands of Irish ecclesiastics and of which a great number have been preserved in Ireland, often kept in precious caskets (Pl. 2).

The Irish missionaries also imposed their art nearer Ireland. The monastery founded by St. Columba on Iona, on the coast of Scotland, which was peopled by Irishmen for centuries, was the starting-point for missions in Scotland and in the North of England, and was at the same time a centre for the diffusion of Irish art. It was from there that the Irish decorative methods were transmitted to Lindisfarne, founded in 635 on the coast of Northumbria. A manuscript coming from Lindisfarne, which is now in the cathedral of Durham (Ms. A. II, 10) shows a stage of Irish miniature work a little more evolved than that represented by the manuscripts of Bobbio; great knots of a broad ribbon determine the framework of the page; they are the same in design, but in each of the colours—blue, red, yellow—they are differently divided up, giving an extraordinary iridescence to the whole of the composition.

At the same time, other Irish monasteries appeared in the South of England, such as that which St. Fursy founded in Norfolk about 634 or 635. This monastery, founded under the auspices of a King of East Anglia and reconstructed by his successors, is probably the origin of the enamel bowls of Irish type which were found in the royal tomb at Sutton Hoo.

But the renewal of contacts with the Continent which allowed for the conversion of England, the continual comings and goings which took place in the VIIth century between Ireland and the continental monasteries, introduced little by little new elements into Irish art, at the same time that its success even abroad and the contact of other arts led it to define itself even more rigorously, to define the special character of what now became a coherent decorative system, with a peculiarly uncompromising method. This system, with its prehistoric taste for covering the surface, its refusal of all realism, its rigorously abstract treatment of the human or animal form, is to be found developing harmoniously in the works which date clearly from the second half of the VIIth century. The great Steles of Inishkea and Fahan Mura, the cross of Cardonagh (Pl. 3B) —the various slabs of stones decorated in very light relief—and the *Book of Durrow*—the most ancient of Irish manuscripts with a large decorative scheme—are the best examples.

Pages of stone and pages of parchment are covered with the close texture of a broad ribbon, touched up in the manuscript with green, yellow and red. In the intervals left by these knots, other decorative motifs have found their place, birds, people, animals borrowed from Saxon gold- and silversmiths' work. In all that, there is a perfect equality of treatment, combined curbs following subtle rhythms, colours which respond to each other and alternate, usually in contradiction to the symmetry. The curved line pre-eminently, the spiral, which was already sketched out in Celtic art, and which had come out distinctly in various works of the Vth and VIth centuries, comes into full play and displays itself widely on one of the carpet pages of the manuscript, in the decoration, now infinitely complex, of the capitals, and on some of the steles.

Among the Irish books which have survived down to our time, the *Book of Durrow* is the oldest to have a really organized decorative programme. At the head of each of the Gospels, we first find a page bearing the symbol of the evangelist (Pl. 3A), then two pages facing each other, to the left a page of ornaments and to the right the beginning of the text, with a large capital occupying almost all the upper part of the page, followed by some words in ornamented letters, on a base of stippling. We shall find this arrangement again, with only a few variants, in all the manuscripts, and especially in a few large Gospel books which are very little later in date than the *Book of Durrow*.

The Gospel books come, for the most part, from Irish monasteries outside Ireland, whether they were taken there, or written and decorated there. The chief ones are the great Gospel book coming from the Abbey of Echternach in Luxembourg (Bibl. Nat.), the Gospel book of St. Chad (Lichfield Cathedral), and the Gospel book of Lindisfarne (British Museum).

There has been much discussion about the manuscripts of Echternach. M. Masai has made of them one of the principal arguments for his theory as to English origin of the " so-called Irish " manuscripts. He has forgotten a little too much in insisting on the fact that the founder of Echternach, Willibrord, was English, for Alcuin, who wrote his life, shows him coming at twenty years old to study in Ireland, and only leaving twelve years later to go and evangelize

Friesland, with a dozen companions of whom some were probably Irish. The library of Echternach contained several manuscripts in the Irish style of which a certain number are now at the Bibliothèque Nationale: a calendar, probably of the time of Willibrord, decorated with capitals with fine spirals, a manuscript of the prophets, in a similar style, but more vehement, the work of a scribe who signs himself Virgilius—probably a latinization of the Irish name Ferghil—then some manuscripts which have found their way into the German collections, of which the chief is the Gospel book of Maihingen, perhaps also written by Virgilius, and essentially Irish, both by the characters of the text and by the delicate and fanciful decoration. Another Gospel book, that of Trèves, in which some continental characters appear, beside interlaced ornaments ribboned in the style of Durrow, and capitals very like those of the Gospel book of Maihingen, is connected with the same group. (Pl. 4A).

But the jewel of this series is the great Gospel book in the possession of the Bibliothèque Nationale. It also has a text which is clearly Irish, and it is possible that it was brought from Ireland. It represents a stage of Irish illumination very little later than the *Book of Durrow,* in which spirals and interlaced ornaments play an essential rôle, the interlaced ornaments often losing their thick ribboned contours to become a network of thin threads, with the spiral unrolling itself giddily; on all this there is a play of infinitely delicate colours, pink, an orange yellow, a citron yellow, purple and mauve.

This clever graduation of colours is to be found again in the great Gospel book coming from Lindisfarne which is kept in the British Museum, but there a new element has been added to the traditional repertory, a decoration made of animals, little quadrupeds or birds, with drawn out bodies which are combined in skilful weaving; they run along the borders, climb the length of the shafts of the letters, and cross each other in complicated and perpetually renewed combinations on the surface of the great carpet pages. The principle even of the animal intertwined ornaments already existed in a page of the *Book of Durrow,* but the animals have changed in aspect: they have taken on a deceptive appearance of reality,—deceptive because they are in fact neither dogs, nor lion cubs, of which some of them have the head, but are indeed fictions of the imagination, malleable, capable of being drawn out, pliable at the will of the artist, as completely submitted to the rhythm as the spiral, interlaced ornaments or the foliage of which they sometimes borrow the appearance. In the Gospel book of Lichfield (which probably came from Ireland into England by the intermediary of a monastery in Gaul), this style reaches a paroxysm: ornaments cover the page, in a net-work which is only limited by certain frames of ribbon in vivid colours, and are animated

by a continuous movement which drags in the frameworks themselves, of which the extremities bristle with hooked paws and devouring heads; the decoration bubbles up with a fantasy that is always
new, but obstinately unreal, impassive, rebellious against any imitation
of the world.

The formula defined in such a masterly way by the painter of the
book of Lichfield has been employed, with only the modifications
due to a different technique, by the gold- and silversmiths and the
sculptors of the VIIIth century. The brooch of Tara (Pl. 5), the
chalice of Ardagh, the great stone crosses at Ahenny (Pl. 6B) and at
Kilkieran are the equivalents of the manuscripts which we have
just examined, with affinities which would deserve to be dwelt upon:
the brooch, with its borders of entangled birds like the links of a
chain and its framework in the form of animals, is more closely
connected with the Gospel book of Lichfield, whereas the cross of
Ahenny, in which interlaced ornaments properly speaking do not
exist, and in which at moments a certain hardness of line reveals
itself, have singular analogies with the Gospel book of Echternach.

This style will only develop itself in the manuscripts of the VIIIth
century and the beginning of the IXth, Gospel book no. 51 of Saint-
Gall (Pl. 4B and 11B), the book of MacRegol, the book of Armagh,
etc., and in the most monumental of them, the book of Kells, takes
on an extraordinary baroque note.

The *Book of Kells* was probably begun in Iona and finished in
Kells, when the monks of Iona, fleeing before the attacks of the
Vikings, took refuge in Ireland. This exuberance perhaps represents
a variant of Irish ornament belonging specially to Iona, for it is to
be found again on the sculptured crosses which survive on the site
of the monastery. On certain pages of the manuscript, the ornament,
almost without changing its repertory, only incorporating in itself
boughs of foliage, is taken with a dizzy movement. In certain pages,
as those which open each of the Gospels, there is an effervescence, a
sort of overflowing of motifs, which are perpetually transforming
themselves one into the other. The limit between spiral, animal and
interlaced ornament no longer exists, each is other by a perpetual
interchange of their appearance. And yet, with all this abundance,
the detail keeps its rigorous clearness; this inextricable complexity
is based on a meticulous definition of all the elements, this apparent
disorder is made of a relentless order. (Pl. 7).

Parallel to this ornamental exuberance a tendency begins to show
itself in the *Book of Kells* to illustrate the text, which is from certain
points of view, the opposite. Manuscript no. 51 of Saint-Gall already
had two pages representing the Crucifixion and the Last Judgment,

treated in a style which remains essentially ornamental and endeavours to respect the intelligibility of the scene.

A manuscript of the library of Turin, coming from Bobbio, and very near in style to the *Book of Kells*, also has figured scenes. In the *Book of Kells* we find a page representing the Virgin and Child, others consecrated to the Temptation and the Arrest of Christ; there would probably have been more if the book had not remained unfinished. Little personages who, running between the lines or who are to be seen sitting on a letter, also clearly have a direct connection with the words which they accompany. (Pl. 8).

These new preoccupations are no doubt an echo of the figurative tendencies which have shown themselves from the beginning of the Carolingian era. M. A. M. Friend has shown that the six first pages of the canons of concordance of the *Book of Kells* are imitated from another manuscript, which has now disappeared, and which also served as a model for a Carolingian manuscript of the Rhenish group going back to the neighbourhood of the year 800. We are at a moment when exchanges are made in both directions, with an extraordinary intensity.

In fact, if Irish art now begins to be inspired by continental models, it is in a contrary sense to that in which the current of influences had made itself felt. Irish art, starting from the first missions on the Continent, had penetrated into Merovingian circles, then into the first Carolingian centres and had, especially in the domain of miniatures, a profound effect. It was made to attract the Merovingian illuminator who was taken with abstract combinations, sometimes inclined to be geometrical to a rather tedious extent, based on the lines of the compasses. But the proof of this attraction is that it maintained itself in the Carolingian circles which were the most imbued with classicism. Irish art presented a variety of motifs, a suppleness in passing from one to the other, resources of strangeness and of the fantastic which attracted the copyists. The picturesque and sometimes comical side of the animal interlaced ornaments, the sense of continued winding, that is what they saw. Its very abstraction, the principles of abstraction which had gone to the elaboration of these monsters, of all this world created on the margin of reality to evoke and to deny it at the same time, that constant elasticity which permitted the Irish artist equally to avoid geometrical crystallization and literal realism, this was missed by many of the copyists. But we must remember that alongside the continental illuminators who imitated an imported manuscript, there were also the scribe-painters who were directly formed by the Irish masters, knowing not only their repertory, but their very principles, and these were able to introduce into the art of the Continent more than a simple decorative routine.

This influence was moreover sporadic, intermittent, and was sometimes a delayed action, with a gap of a century or two between the model and his imitators. It has all sorts of nuances and variations of which we can only indicate a few, and which have been studied in detail by G. L. Micheli in his book on the influence of Irish miniature work.

We have seen the first stage of this history, and the apparition of the Irish style in the monasteries of St. Columban. Echternach, at the beginning of the VIIIth century, is another case of massive penetration by Irish models, brought, this time, by a mixed group of Saxon and Irish missionaries. During the whole of the VIIIth century, the Irish missionaries, pilgrims, travellers, visited the Continent, stayed in the old foundations of their island, brought their books and kept them in contact with Ireland. It was not merely Saint-Gall or Bobbio, where the Irishman Cummean came to die, but many other insular centres. Péronne—*Peronna Scottorum*—of which the monastery preserved the tomb of the Irishman Fursy, was without doubt one of the most important, and its influence seems to have radiated over all the North of Gaul; Fluery-sur-Loire, Tours under the abbacy of Alcuin who had been brought up as the pupil of an Irishman in York, Flavigny, are all equally beset with Irish models. In Germany, the monastery of Wurzburg, founded in the VIth century, by the Irishman Kilian, Salzburg where there taught in the middle of the VIIIth century the Irishman Virgil of Salzburg, were also centres for the importation and diffusion of manuscripts. Hybrid continental styles developed, which had their lapses, but the number and variety of which show the extraordinary popularity of the models. One would like to know in greater detail the scriptoria, like those of the monasteries of Laon and of Corbie (Pl. 9B), and that of Flavigny. And this all the more in that the influences, as we have already noted, work in the same direction. Among the manuscripts of the Laon-Corbie group, there is one which is now kept in the cathedral at Essen, of which one page bears a striking likeness to the last page of St. Mark's Gospel in the *Book of Kells*. (Pl. 9A). As for the manuscripts of Flavigny, which have taken on quite a new significance since it has been possible to connect them with the Sacramentary of Gellone, they represent an astonishing group in which the insular influence shows itself clearly by the use of certain decorative motifs and stipplings, but in which everything is worked out with a fundamental originality and which has been able to lend as well as to borrow: There is a remarkable similarity of method between the capitals made of a combination of animals in the Sacramentary, and those of the *Book of Kells* or the *Book of Armagh*. But in most cases, the system is worked out with an absolutely different accent.

Everywhere there are imitations with more or less success of the animal interlaced ornaments, great knots of interlaced ornament, even in the composition of a page. Where, however, these borrowings are specially striking, is when they show themselves in surroundings which at first sight might have been expected to be hostile to them: the scriptoria of the Rhine valley working for the imperial court. The close relations with the classical model, the imitation of motifs borrowed directly from Mediterranean manuscripts, the use of characters in gold and silver on a purple base, all this seems a bad preparation for those great monumental capitals which are most directly imitated from Irish manuscripts, and from fairly old manuscripts, preserved in the region for nearly a century, such as the Gospel book of Echternach or that of Trèves. The Gospel books which were ordered by Charlemagne and his court all have these imposing letters flowering with interlaced ornaments; one part of the fantasy of the model has disappeared, as well as the more unruly elements of the decoration, both spiral and animal, but the appearance of the whole remains the same and clearly shows the source of inspiration. (Pl. 10).

This rather paradoxical intrusion into an art which set out to be classical, may have its explanation in the presence of numerous Irishmen at the court of Charlemagne and his successors, which was able to create a fashion and to turn the curiosity of these painters towards these unexpected models. Certain of them, like the geographer Dicuil and Clement, who succeeded Alcuin at the Palace School, came perhaps attracted simply by the welcome which the Emperor kept for men of learning. But with the ninth century there begins a new phase of Irish journeys on the Continent. They were now refugees, fleeing before the invasion of the Vikings, who came to find asylum in the old foundations of the Continent and at the hands of the imperial protectors. All the great monasteries of the island had suffered. Armagh and Clonmacnois were almost destroyed. Iona was sacked, and its monks came to take shelter in Ireland, at Kells.

The monks of Lindisfarne, after also having tried, as it would seem, to go to Ireland, wandered for a time, with their relics and their most precious manuscripts, and ended by establishing themselves at Durham. Many others, however, sought for refuge further

---

² The round towers which are one of the most striking features of Irish monastic ruins, probably appear at this period. They served at the same time as bell-towers (the little hand bell was rung through the windows which always existed below the roof), as watch-towers and as keeps where the community could in case of danger take refuge with its precious objects.

afield. Sedulius Scottus established himself at Liège in 848, Scotus Eriugena taught at the Palace School from 845 till about 870, and crowds of learned men and less well-known scribes arrived during the first half of the century at Péronne, Saint-Riquier and Laon. They came with their books, of which some carry in their marginal notes the memory of this exodus, while others were written in the continental monasteries. Their presence brought about a renewal of interest in the insular style, a sort of rejuvenation of its influence.

The style which is usually called Franco-Insular, which had probably had as its centre the monastery of Saint-Amand, of which the Abbot, Hucbald, was the pupil of an Irishman, was certainly the result of this new afflux. It had a great vogue in the North of France, and in the region of Liège and Cologne; but its radiance stretched much further, to Southern Germany, to Bobbio, where it found the ground all prepared for it, and from there it played its rôle in the formation of the Beneventine miniature.

There, in spite of the gold, and the monumental ordering of the pages, which continues the style of the great Gospel books which had gone before, something of the impetuosity of the best phase of Irish miniature reappears. Alongside the interlaced ornaments, the spiral and the foundation of stipplings a whole world of agile and firmly drawn little animals fill the prongs of the letters and their intervals. The second Bible of Charles the Bald, the Gospel book of Francis II, the Gospel book of Arras, are the most striking examples of this new adaptation of the Irish style. (Pl. 11A).

Up to now we have only examined the diffusion of the Irish style in the manuscripts. One can wonder whether Irish gold and silver work had a similar influence. In fact, we are faced with very few Irish objects found on the Continent; an enamelled bowl found near the mouth of the Meuse (Leyden museum) and the fragment of another found in Belgium (Cinquantenaire museum). That is all, if one leaves aside objects found in excavations in Scandinavia, which, brought back by the Viking expeditions to Ireland, certainly had an effect on the development of their art, but that is outside the scope of this study. The museum at Saint-Germain possesses two objects in gilded bronze, coming from the Victor Gay collection, which are certainly of Irish fabrication, but as Gay left no indication as to their origin, it is impossible to place them. It is possible, however, that travelling monks brought with them some metal objects, and besides at that period metal work is so closely tributary to that of illumination that it would be astonishing to find no echo of the Irish style.

In reality, there is a whole group of objects coming from Germany, Austria and Switzerland which are decorated with a network of slender animals, covering part of the surface. The most remarkable is probably a chalice bearing the name of Tassilo, Duke of Bavaria, which belongs to the monastery of Kremsmünster. One sees, as on other objects of the period, interlaced ornaments and interlaced animal ornaments made of rather disjointed little quadrupeds. They are not strictly speaking Irish ornaments but near relations to those beasts of a rather hesitating and simplified structure which one finds in a fairly large number of continental manuscripts imitating Irish or Irish-Saxon models. The whole group seems to be a derivation from the insular art such as one finds in the manuscripts. Other objects, like the reliquary of Coire, also seem very close to Irish inspiration, which is not surprising, so near to Saint-Gall.

Did this engrossing passion for Irish motifs extend to the decoration of monuments ? What we know of the early Middle Ages offers more fallacious parallels with insular art than genuine imitations. It would no doubt be idle to seek in the interlaced ornaments of the chancel plaques, which from Lombardy are spread over part of Gaul, Switzerland, Dalmatia, etc., for anything else than a derivation from oriental or perhaps Roman models parallel to that which was produced in Ireland, and often rejoining it on account of the monotony of combinations inherent in the motif itself. The fact that examples are to be found at Bobbio and at Coire is not enough for ascribing to them an insular origin. But where the problem becomes more disturbing is when, in the monastery of Münster, on one of the roads which can lead from Saint-Gall and Coire to the valley of the Po, these interlaced ornaments are accompanied by animals clearly derived from Irish models. The two great pillars preserved in the church of Cravant (Indre-et-Loire), whose interlaced ornaments have an accentuated relief and an irregularity of outline not usually to be found in the Lombard style, do not fail to suggest the intervention of an Irish model (Pl. 6A) or even the hand of a travelling sculptor. But before venturing further on this delicate subject of sculpture, we should return to Ireland to look at what has happened from this point of view during the IXth and Xth centuries.

Irish art of that period is chiefly known to us by sculptures. Illumination rapidly degenerated, probably on account of the departure of a large number of the painters. Once, however, that the violence of the Scandinavian attacks had abated, and that a little tranquillity returned to the devastated monasteries, large sculptured crosses arose on all sides. They have the same aspect as those of the VIIIth century, and seem to have been set up here and there among conventual buildings. But their decoration is changed. To the old ornamental themes are added Biblical scenes which soon cover the greater part of the surface. The most ancient of these crosses, which must have been set up at Kells at the time of the foundation of the monastery, shows about the same juxtaposition of sculpture narrative and pure ornament as the *Book of Kells* whose decoration no doubt came to an end at about the same time. During the whole of the IXth century a series of experiments were attempted, by sculptors who were seeking to combine and to reconcile the two elements. Some of them, like the sculptor of the cross of Moone Abbey, achieved this by making their personages combinations of geometrical figures. (Pl. 12). Others discreetly introduced into the scenes repre sented souvenirs of the form of the interlaced ornaments and ol the spiral, to which they submitted their personages. But all were now concerned with the readability of the episode represented. Their sources of information must have been very varied. Sometimes they were clearly oriental—pages of manuscripts or small portable objects —sometimes the composition is curiously like that of Carolingian ivories. And in view of the quite new concern to model the per- sonages in high relief, we must also see an imitation of the style of the ivories.

These sculptures, carved in a sandstone which wears away very easily, are often no more than the shadow of themselves. But some crosses, like that of Abbot Muiredach at Monasterboice (Pl. 14) which an inscription dates from the beginning of the Xth century, have preserved a certain delicacy, and the finer shades of original work. A detailed study of the iconography of these columns would set many problems—the Last Judgment of the cross of Muiredach, for example, of which certain elements seem to come directly from the Egyptian books of the dead, but which at the same time, with the scene of the weighing of the souls, joins up with Roman art and the Last Judgment of the doorway at Autun.

To point this out is to raise a problem which can only be approached with plenty of hesitations, that of the part played by the art that we have just been examining, and by its diffusion on the Continent, in the elaboration of Roman art. In reality the problem has two aspects: on the one hand Roman art was born in a milieu still impregnated with Irish traditions and methods. We find our- selves here and there in the face of experiments, like the capitals of the Gospel book of Metz of the Xth century, the great Aquitanian manuscripts of the XIth century, in which there lives again, not a stock of garnishings of Irish decoration which have rather lost their freshness, but the actual spirit which in the VIIIth century had elaborated the new motif of animal interlaced ornament, starting from the theme of interlaced ornament and the spiral. In the capitals of the Gospel book of Metz, where the symbol of the evangelist is boldly bent to fit in with the outline of the letter, semi-realist figures are employed, but they are subjected to impossible movements which have, however, a note of probability, their structure being decided by that of the letter. It is indeed the system in which the little Lindisfarnian greyhound was drawn out and bent to the form of interlaced ornament or an acanthus. But it is also, in germ, all the principle from which the statue-column would emerge, or the figures on Roman spandrels dragged along by the lines of the composition. The first Bible of Limoges would furnish similar examples which would lead to the pier of Souillac and to so many contests of Roman animals. We are led to suspect that Roman sculptors sometimes used insular manuscripts by the details which suddenly appear here and there, a border of devouring animals, for example, as has been pointed out by M. Vallery Radot at Lyons, on two capitals at Carennac (Pl. 15), the one decorated with an animal interlaced ornament, the other bearing, alongside the interlaced ornament, a person carrying two branches, like the one who appears at the base of a page of the *Book of Kells,* or the Christ in Judgment of the great Irish crosses. (Pl. 13).

The other aspect of the problem is the fact that the great Irish crosses represent a sort of preliminary experiment in Roman art, a first rough outline in stone of many of the themes that were to be taken up again. Did contacts also take place there? Did Irish sculptors also come on the Continent like the scribes and the painters ? It is difficult to say The art of the great crosses disappeared towards the end of the Xth century, to be replaced by an art in which ornament suddenly reconquered almost all the territory it had lost. The decoration of the Roman-Irish churches is also almost completely ornamental. Will it ever be possible to decide if the sculptors of the great crosses were only the predecessors of Roman art or really its precursors ?

The Coffret of Mortain

By CHANOINE BLOUET
Honorary Archpriest of Mortain

At Mortain a small chest guards the memory of the great Irish saints, conquerors for Christ in France. (Pl. 16).

THE migrations of peoples and the great currents of ideas leave behind them some witnesses which, long centuries later, astonish those who discover them. Such is the case with the *Coffret* (small chest) or *Chrismale,* in the sacristy at Mortain, in La Manche, a unique and very little known souvenir of the influence in the West of France of the great Irish monks of the Vth and VIth centuries.

The little chest, which is of very small dimensions (0.135 metres in length, 0.050 metres in breadth, 0.12 metres in height), consists of a box of beechwood, hollowed out and lined with a sheet of embossed and gilded copper. With these humble proportions the little object refracts like some marvellous prism, the rays of four or five civilizations.

In its little town of Lower Normandy, in the isolation of a sacristy, it has known long centuries of silent life. In 1865 a local scholar, the mayor of the neighbourhood, M. Henri Moulin, described it and pointed out the strangeness of its runic inscription; in 1870, an archaeologist drew it; in 1899 an editor, Le Masle of Le Havre, photographed it; in 1905 the authorities of the *Beaux-Arts* inscribed it among the historic monuments; in 1923, Chanoine Delaporte attracted the attention of Maurice Cahen who came to study it on the spot; in 1927, Magnus Olsen, the celebrated professor of Oslo, came in his turn to verify the runes and to confirm the judgment of the young French scholar who had been snatched by death the previous year from his learned career. And these specialists in philology soon learnt, by the work in common of Cahen, Olsen and Andler, that the little chest of Mortain was in fact: " the only example which has come down to us of what the lives of the Irish saints call a Chrismale."

On its front face the *Coffret of Mortain* presents the image of Christ as Pantocrator, accompanied by the archangels Michael and Gabriel, with a third angel on the centre of the lid. The Christ who holds a book and the archangels who hold a sphere, make at the same time the gesture of blessing. At the back, on the roof, there is an inscription of eighteen runic characters of which a text in ancient Anglo-Saxon has been deciphered by Cahen and Olsen: *" May God aid Eada, he made this Chrismale."*

How many, among us, have seen a runic inscription? This alphabet is as foreign to us as that of the old Etruscans. And yet the Anglo-Saxons and the Scandinavians used these characters for long centuries, right down to the commencement of the Middle Ages. In England, in Germany, in the Northern countries, specialists study them eagerly; in France, M. Fernand Mossé occupies at the Collège de France Maurice Cahen's chair, and continues his work. After many discussions they seem to have come to know its origins. Coming from the Latin it evolved in order to express the sounds of the Anglo-Saxon languages; it is angular and would seem to have been at first carved with a knife on the bark of the trees. A very curious thing is that the present state of our knowledge allows us to date a runic text from the form of its characters.

In thus comparing the *Coffret de Mortain* with the Frankish casket in the British Museum, another little whalebone box found more than a century ago at Auzon, near Clermont-Ferrand, at the Glaive de la Tamise, and to Alcuin's manuscript, which all bear runic inscriptions, Cahen and Olsen placed the text of Mortain between 660 and 725.

The most remarkable thing yet is that this inscription reveals to us the origin and destiny of the *Coffret*. These runes come from Northumbria, in direct dependence on the famous Abbey of Iona and Irish Christianity. The object is not a reliquary, but a Chrismale, destined to carry when travelling the Body of Christ. We thus meet the direct influence of the great Irish saints Columban, Columba and Comgall. What a marvellous cycle of legend! St. Comgall was working in the fields, with the *Chrismale* on his chest; the *Chrismale* put to flight the robbers who were hanging round. In Ireland, in Wales, in Northumbria, and perhaps in French Brittany, monks and priests accompanied bands of travellers carrying before them the Body of Christ in a *Chrismale*.

How did this relic, so clearly belonging to the Irish liturgy, come to take refuge at Mortain, " in that little town of Lower Normandy ", as Olsen says? The first hypothesis to be pointed out rests on the intimate relations which united Ireland and the West of France in the VIth and VIIth centuries. Everyone knows how saints from Ireland and from Gaul came in order to evangelize Brittany; Father Bernard Jacqueline, a young and brilliant Norman scholar, draws our attention to the fact that most of the ancient saints of the diocese of Contances are also of Irish origin.

The most plausible hypothesis is that of a gift of the Norman princes, William the Conqueror and Robert, Count of Mortain, to the collegiate church of this town founded by them after the conquest of England. Normandy awoke at this time beneath a rain of gifts: ciboriums, chalices and precious manuscripts. Down to these last years, the collegiate church at Mortain still preserved a Gospel book of English origin which came in the same way. And the *Chrismale* bearing the effigies of the angels Michael and Gabriel had its place all ready in the country where there flourished an ardent devotion to the archangel St. Michael, in the radiance of the celebrated Benedictine abbey.

The men of our time are even more struck by the artistic and theological lights which come from the *Coffret of Mortain*. Its composition is clearly connected with Roman and Ravenna mosaics, with coptic sculptures and with the celebrated Irish manuscripts, such as the *Book of Kells*, the most beautiful book in the world, as the Irish say. From the doctrinal point of view it presents to us Christ in glory, encircled with angels and giving the blessing with them. The German archaeologist Wulf sees in this arrangement of figures an allusion to Abraham's vision of angels and in fact a trinitarian symbol.

A meeting-place of ideas and of civilizations, the *Coffret of Mortain* is a great Christian document which up to now has remained more or less unknown. Its history is connected with the great Celtic and Norman epic poems; its mystical quality is penetrated with a radiance of fraternal love which is truly universal. It is to go on a fervent pilgrimage to the past that the little vessel of beech-wood and copper invites us; like the caravels of the Trophées, it will cause to be—
" Set up for us in an unknown sky
   New stars from the depth of the ocean[1]."

---

[1] *Monter en un ciel ignoré*
Du fond de l'océan des étoiles nouvelles.